Strawcraft
and
Corn Dollies

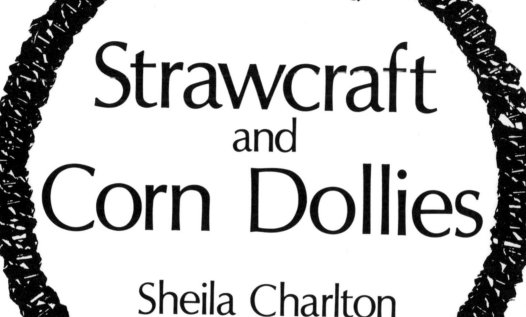

Strawcraft
and
Corn Dollies

Sheila Charlton

photographs by Stan Charlton
and drawings by Michael Woods

Blandford Press London

This book was designed and produced by
Alphabet and Image, Sherborne, Dorset.

First published by Blandford Press Ltd 1974

Typeset by Specialised Offset Services Ltd, Liverpool
Printed and bound in Great Britain by Redwood Burn Ltd,
Trowbridge & Esher

ISBN: 0 7137 0693 6

Contents

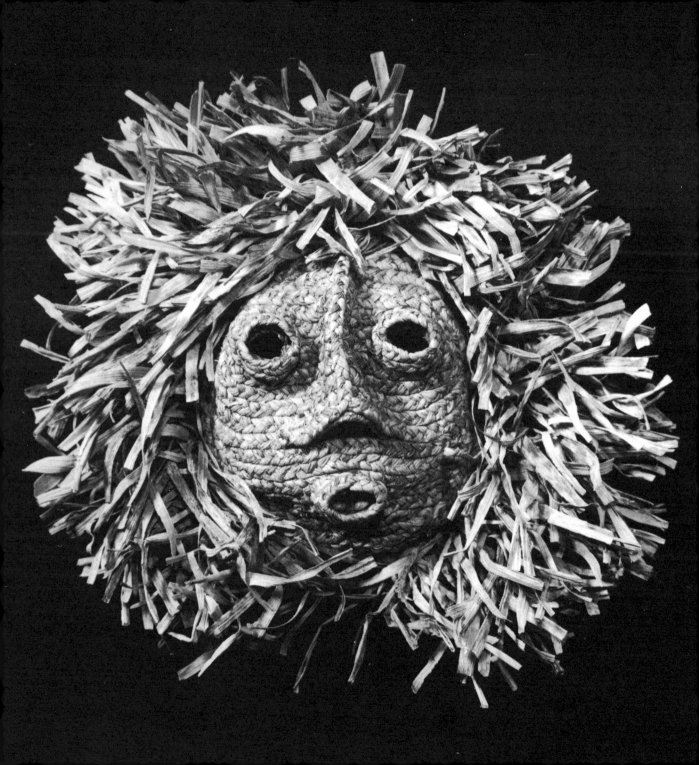

1 Corn Idols

'An old man ... when the labourers are reaping the last field of wheat ... goes round to the shocks and the sheaves and picks out a little bundle of all the best ears he can find; this bundle he ties up very neat and trim, and plaits and arranges the straws very tastefully .... After the field is cut out, and the pitcher once more circulated, the reapers, binders and women stand round in a circle.' There follows a solemn ceremony, with chants and loud cries: 'a neck! a neck!' The place is Devon, England. The time, the middle of the last century. The plaited corn could be one of several spiralling shapes, and the ceremony — well, there are countless variations. The object of the exercise can be explained according to one's belief. It is either a communal get-together where hard physical labour has produced visibly successful results, a thanksgiving within the Christian Church for good crops and good weather, or the vestiges of a superstitious ritual to appease the goddess of the corn.

Similar ceremonies, with similar corn idols, are recorded not only in all corners of Britain, Scandinavia, Germany and France, but amongst the Indians of Peru and Mexico and the natives of Burma, Java and the Celebes. Wherever, in fact, the sun is warm enough to ripen crops, corn and its source were at some time worshipped. Perhaps for the worshipper the ritual was self-explanatory. The Greeks, for example, celebrated Demeter, the

Left A husk face or 'bushy head' as made by North American Indians from shredded and braided maize husks, for use at the midwinter festival.

7

fertile mother goddess, at the Spring sowing, and the same corn was reincarnated as a daughter goddess, Persephone, by harvest time. The Romans simplified these beliefs slightly by worshipping Ceres as the goddess of crops all through the year.

The following passage from *Happy Days in Norway* by Sigrid Undset, translated by E.R. Wood, illustrates the belief in the power of the god or spirit of the corn in the last sheaf to be cut.

Many thousand years ago when the Stone Age men in Norway had learnt to cultivate corn they thought that the power of growth that lived in the earth escaped when they cut their fields and hid itself in the last corn that remained standing. When that too had been cut, they had captured the spirit of growth. They therefore kept this last corn sheaf and laid it aside.

At midwinter when the earth lay frost-bound and decked with snow, when there came sinister rumblings at night from the ice on the sea, and the trees in the wood cracked with cold . . . Then the Stone Age people fetched this last sheaf of corn and hung it out near their dwelling places. The power in it was said to help the sun to become refreshed again so that it could give warmth and light and overcome the evil winter. Then the spirit of growth might fly home again to the thawed-out fields and bring the people a new harvest of blessed corn.

It is the corn goddess or the life-giving spirit of the corn which is essentially the prototype for all the symbolic corn dollies made from Egyptian times to the present day. Add to this the tendency of corn to look decorative when arranged in an orderly fashion, and its habit of turning into a regular spiral form when plaited, and most of the contents of this book can be blamed on history. Modern-day plaiters are not, as far as I know, trying to appease anything, and it is ironical that this decorative craft, which started as an urgent and compulsive need to create and celebrate, should flourish today when

mechanization and leisure tend to separate the straw-worker from the corn.

The primitive farmer, like the child who asks what makes seeds grow into plants, sought a simple solution to the mystery of growth. Since gods are invoked to account for mysteries, there had to be a spirit or god of corn (or rather a goddess, for procreation is the province of the female). Some thought that she lived in the field, others that she dwelt in the corn itself. Gods and spirits were considered more capricious, more benevolent, more cruel, and above all more powerful than any man. They were to be pandered to and given the proper respect through rites and ceremonies in the hope that they would be favourably disposed to bring about the annual miracle necessary for the next harvest.

Man usually makes images of gods or goddesses in human shape and the oldest form of corn idol or 'dolly' is probably the Corn Mother or the Corn Maiden, depending upon the interpretation: either she is the mother carrying the fruit of her maturity or the maiden bearing seed but not yet brought to fruition. A collection of corn dollies based on the human figure would include several basic types with some variations as worked by particular craftsmen. Most straw-workers sooner or later attempt to make a human-form dolly and a fine example of the whole-sheaf doll is the modern Ceres by Lettice Sandford, shown on page 11. A whole-sheaf dolly can be evocative, even slightly sinister-looking, and stands up to 4 feet high. In its crudest form arms were added merely by tying in bunches of corn at right angles to the main sheaf. This was later decorated, perhaps from the hedgerows as the Kentish name 'Ivy Girl' suggests, or by plaits and braids of straw. By the addition of braids a figure developed more personality, then a waist and then an elaborate coiffure with plaited hair. She was sometimes dressed in a gown of paper, rags or even cotton, as in the Kern Maiden of Scotland.

Although the plaits would have been made early in the day, probably while the dew was on the corn, the sheaf used for this dolly was traditionally the last to be cut. When cut the harvesters would assemble to celebrate the completed task with a joyful procession. The horses drawing the loaded cart would be decorated with ribbons and corn and perched on the last load would be a young girl chosen as Harvest Queen, sitting side-by-side with the decorated sheaf representing Ceres. On such an occasion the harvest doll would be taken into the barn or village hall and would have pride of place at the harvest supper — but not all corn effigies were honoured in this way. Sometimes the last sheaf was plaited in situ, and hooked down by the reapers from a distance, hurling their sickles at it. The first to bring it down in this exhibitionist way would race back to the farm with it, whilst others would try to douse him and the corn with water — invoking next year's rain.

Some farms would proudly display the plaited trophy or 'neck' from year to year in the farmhouse, whilst in other regions this last sheaf, or the dolly made from it, was a bogey, to be left on another's farm where harvesting was still incomplete. In Herefordshire, the cry of 'the mare! the mare!' would ring out when reaping was over. The last sheaf was tied into the shape of a mare before being cut, and the cutting was another competition in the skill of sickle throwing, all the men lining up at the side of the field to take aim. Whoever was successful in severing the corn seized it and carried it off to a neighbouring field as an insult to those still working. Of course, the recipients were not eager to have it, and if the man was seen every effort was made to prevent him delivering it, or to drench him with water. Once the mare had arrived, however, work was speeded up so that it could be carried off to another unfinished harvest, and nobody wanted the doubtful honour of being the last to finish cutting.

The belief that this last sheaf held an evil spirit was so strong in some places that it was buried in a grave or never cut at all but trampled back into the ground, or the sickles were thrown at it so that no-one should know who cut it and the spirit would be too confused to wreak vengeance.

Right Harvest Maid, a whole-sheaf dolly by Lettice Sandford

2 Straws and Ears

Imagine a cornfield in August, with the crop ready for reaping but the ears not ripe enough for threshing. Imagine cutting a sheaf of long-strawed corn, stripping off the flag or leaf and plaiting the fresh, strong pliable straws directly into a corn maiden with no preparation, and no tools. Such straw is perfect for plaiting.

You have to imagine all this, because as strawcraft becomes more and more popular the combination of the right material and the right conditions become ever more rare. The combine harvester cuts the modern short-strawed wheat when it is a little past its best for plaiting, and breaks and smashes the straw in the threshing process so that it is no more use to the plaiter than it is to the thatcher.

It is natural enough that the straw-worker will be the last person to be considered in the economics of farming, and what used to be an abundant by-product at any harvest time now has to be sought out with care and skill. Some expert plaiters claim that the corn should be cut when it is green, so that the seeds do not fall out too readily. I find this advantage offset by the amount of pith remaining in the stem, making joining more difficult. The best corn is to be had by cutting just before the farmer harvests.

The best straw for plaiting is wheat, and the best wheat is that which has a long stem and a fine colour. The farmer will choose a wheat for its high yield, its disease resistance and, amongst other things, the shortness of its straw, and it is for this reason that such good plaiting varieties as *Squarehead Master* are hard to find. Good straw will not taper too rapidly towards the ear, and will have a good cavity through the stem. The widely-grown variety *Capelle* is used by some plaiters, but I find that *Maris Widgeon* and Spring-sown *Kolibri* are my personal favourites amongst wheat.

The ears of corn are part of the beauty of the dolly, and they vary widely in their form. The dollies I have seen in Greece have dark whiskery ears not unlike barley. Barley, rye and oats all have whiskery heads, but for the plaiter their straw is inferior to that of wheat. Barley straw is difficult to handle, as it is fine and bends too easily, though it has a fine silver sheen by comparison with the gold of wheat. Oat straw has a good cavity and a deep golden colour, but it does not easily keep its shape. It is the best material to use if the straw has to be flattened (see Chapter 9) but the beginner's first aim should be a supply of good wheat straw.

Country dwellers will find this easier than those who live in the town, but the first stage will be to approach a farmer *before* harvest time and get his help or at least his approval. With two trespassing footsteps in a wheat field you can damage more growing corn than you will use for plaiting. Most farmers will take an interest in your craft, and will supply you with what you need. Ask him for permission to cut a little corn along the edge of a field where the harvester could have difficulty in reaping. The cost of buying a few hundred straws from the farmer will be very little.

As the craft has gained followers so certain farmers have started to grow corn specifically for the plaiter, and they advertise supplies in some of the daily papers at harvest time. This may well help the town-dweller who has no time to seek out a helpful farmer, but buying straw by post is not the only alternative way of getting materials.

It is quite possible to grow all you need in a small garden.

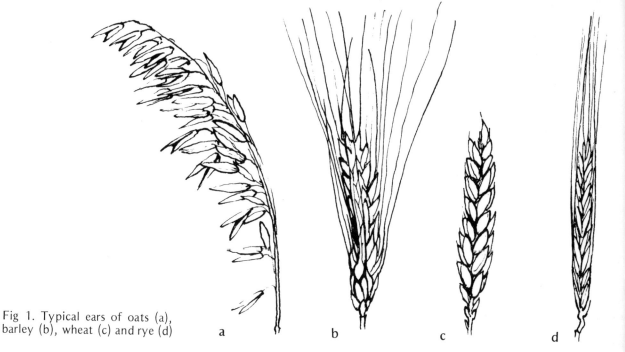

Fig 1. Typical ears of oats (a), barley (b), wheat (c) and rye (d)

a   b   c   d

Two square yards of ground, well dug, with a sprinkling of general fertilizer and sown with 4 oz. of seed will be adequate. The farmer would sow more thinly, but a block of corn is less likely to be blown down in a garden patch if it is thickly sown. Some netting may be required against birds after sowing, and again when the seed heads form. Seeds for Spring wheat like Kolibri can be bought from farm seed suppliers.

This is no help to the town dweller with no garden, and no friendly farmer. He should find out from a library if his county has a guild of craftsmen, which may well include straw plaiters who could help him to find a source. He could also find out if there is a thatcher locally, who may be able to supply him with a sheaf of 'combed reed'. This thatching straw from which the seed has been threshed is not usually too bruised for plaiting, and it should include enough usable ears for dolly decoration.

The organization which manufactures dollies for sale at Cheddar in Somerset also produces a kit of materials with sufficient straw to make four traditional dollies. The kit costs about

£2 ($5) and is available from many craft shops or direct from Somerset House Wedmore, Station Road, Cheddar, Somerset.

If all else fails the frustrated plaiter can practise with an artificial material. Modern drinking straws have some of the same properties as their natural original, and long paper straws costing only a few pence a pack are sold in craft and games shops under the name of Art Straws. The makers do not claim that they are a substitute for corn, but designs taken from corn dollies can certainly be made with them, using the same techniques.

It is disheartening to be faced with a long list of requirements, expensive to buy or difficult to get. Luckily the straw-worker needs little other than straw and nimble fingers. The other requirements are:

> secateurs (straw blunts scissors very quickly)
> thread or thin string, neutral in colour
> gift ribbon for decorative bows in red, green, gold or blue
> string in a strong colour for binding
> fuse wire — 10 or 15 amp

A beginner, using a hundred or so straws, will not need a great deal of any of these tying materials.

Preparing the straw

The straw used for plaiting is the portion from the top of the ear to the first node or joint in the stem. Cut the stem just above the node, and strip off the leaf blade or flag. The lower part of the stem can then be discarded, but as this can produce quite a mess about the place, it is perhaps as well here to outline the method I use to avoid chaos in the house.

I slip the sheaf or bundle into a plastic sack so that the ears and part of the straw protrude from the top. The stems are then withdrawn one by one and cut, leaving the unwanted parts in the sack. I tie the prepared stems into bundles of 50 or 60 straws, taking care that the tie does not bite into the straw. Wire and paper garden ties are useful for this, or 1 inch bandage, which is much better than string.

A bundle of 50 straws will make one, two or more dollies, depending on their size, and it is advisable to grade the bundles so that each contains straws of the same diameter. Once bundled, the straws can be stored indefinitely if they are kept dry and in a mouseproof place.

Dampening the straw

Any straw which is not plaited direct from the cornfield will need conditioning before use.

Wrap the straws you are going to use in an old towel and immerse them in cold water for an hour. Then take them out of the water, but keep in the towel for a further four hours. The straw is now ready for use — slightly damp and pliable. If you are working in a warm room, it is best to keep the straw in a damp wrapping.

The timing is not critical, but if the straws are left in a damp towel for more than twelve hours they will blacken and go mouldy, or even begin to sprout, and so any straw left after a working session should be allowed to dry out before re-storing.

The beginner will soon learn how much straw he needs to prepare for a working session, and in that way will avoid waste. He will also learn how important it is that the straw is in precisely the right condition for plaiting. It is very annoying when plaits split because the straw is too dry.

3 Straw Plaits

The Three-straw plait

Straw behaves quite differently from tresses of human hair, but the simplest straw plait of all is exactly the same as the one every little girl and most little boys learn at primary school. Just in case you have forgotten, it is 'right over centre, left over centre, right over centre', and so on until you run out of material. Three long straws of equal length and size, tied at their ears, can be most easily plaited if flat on a table or similar surface and the resulting braid is flat in section. It is not easy to add new straws inconspicuously when you run out of material, and these simple braids are best used as cords for hanging more complicated dollies.

To tell the truth, they are rather dull, and the beginner can confidently skip over them, although figures are given alongside to make the technique quite clear.

The Four-straw plait

There is more satisfaction in making a plait out of four straws. The result is three-dimensional — more like a rope than a braid. It is quickly learned and a traditional dolly can be made using this technique alone.

Take four well-matched straws of equal length if possible —

Figs 2 and 3. How to make the three-straw plait

Left Typical countryman's favours

19

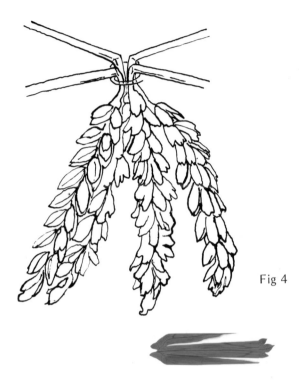

Fig 4

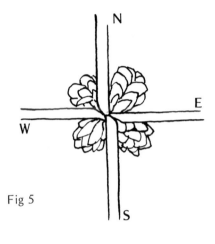

Fig 5

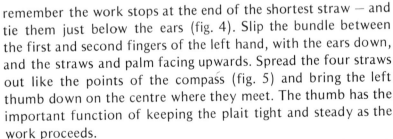

remember the work stops at the end of the shortest straw — and tie them just below the ears (fig. 4). Slip the bundle between the first and second fingers of the left hand, with the ears down, and the straws and palm facing upwards. Spread the four straws out like the points of the compass (fig. 5) and bring the left thumb down on the centre where they meet. The thumb has the important function of keeping the plait tight and steady as the work proceeds.

With the right hand bring the north straw down to the south position, and move the south straw up to the north. Now press down with the thumb. Move east straw to west, and west straw to east. Press down again with the thumb. Now repeat the process, always moving the straws in the same order — N to S, E to W — that's all there is to it. A flexible rather jagged plait will result.

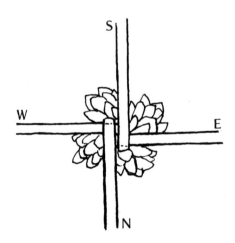

Fig 6. The four-straw plait

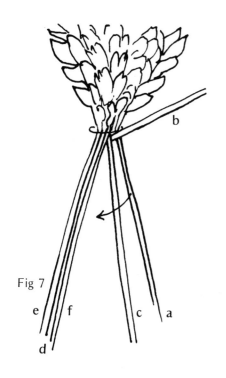

Fig 7

e   f   c   a

d

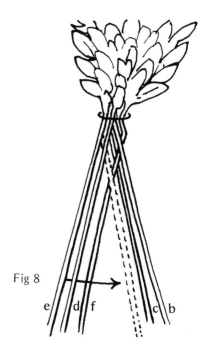

Fig 8

e d f   c b

The Five-straw plait

This time tie five heads together, and lay them down on a flat surface with three straws to one side, two straws to the other. Move straw **a** under **b** and over **c** to lie at **f**. Fig. 7 shows the arrangement. Now move straw **e** under **d** and over the straw at **f** to lie next to **c**. Repeat the movement, always taking the outer straw under its neighbour and over the next one, and working alternately one side and then the other. The result will be another flat braid, like the three-straw plait, but it is wider and more interesting, for it shows more pattern; it is of the kind used in straw hats.

By adding a further two straws, and working the active straw under and over its neighbour alternately, a seven-straw flat braid can also be made. Using nine straws makes for tedious work.

All these plaits are completed by tying the ends together, and trimming off the surplus straws.

21

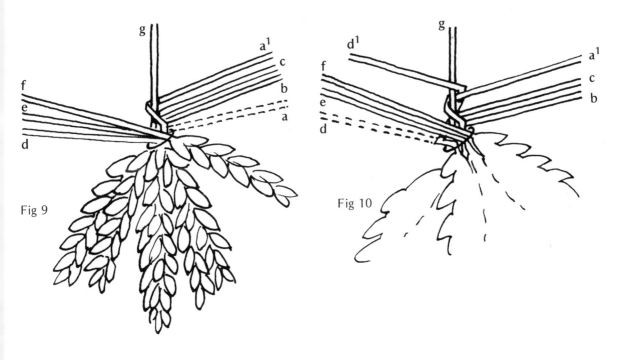

Fig 9

Fig 10

The Seven-straw round plait

A seven-straw plait can be made with a round cross-section. It makes an attractive pattern like a chain, and has many uses in strawcraft.

Tie seven straws together below the ears and arrange them, ears downwards, with one in the centre and three on each side.

1. Take a straw **a** in front of straw **g** (fig. 9) and round the back to lie at a^1.
2. Bring straw **d** *behind* **e**, **f** and **g** and then across *in front of* the centre straw to lie at d^1 (fig. 10).
3. Now bring **b** across the front and round the back of **g** to lie above a^1.
4. Take **e** round behind and then across the front of **g** to lie above d^1.

Fig 11. A simple design using a seven-straw round plait.

5. Take **c** across the front and round the back of **g** to lie above the other straws on the right.
6. Bring **f** behind **g** and across the front to lie above the other straws to the left.

Continue working in this way, taking the bottom straw from each side to the top until you reach the end of the straws. The rope-like plait can be seen in fig. 11 twisted into a circle. Its own ears have been cut off and another bunch added with a ribbon at the join.

The length of the plait is governed by the length of the straw, and will rarely exceed 6 inches. If longer chains are required, then straws must be joined as described in Chapter 5, keeping the joins at the back of the work.

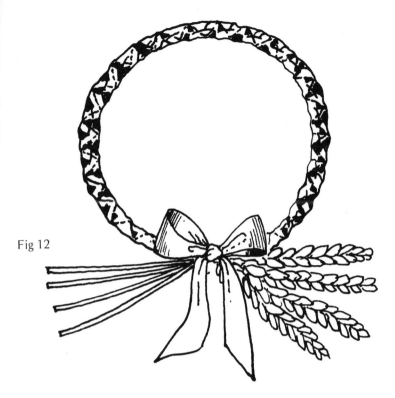

Fig 12

Fig 13

Designs using plaits

Simple plaits can be twisted and joined with ribbons into an enormous variety of shapes. The plaiting technique does not impose a design upon the plaiter, as is the case with some of the spiral dollies, and the inventive beginner can give his imagination full rein.

A three-dimensional design such as a crown or coronet made entirely of plaits can be striking and handsome, but if too many elements are introduced the design can easily become confused. Symmetrical patterns are best, and the plaiter will soon find that a plait becomes stiffer as well as more dynamic when bent into a curve. No doubt this is why many traditional 'favours' made of plaits trimmed with ribbons are circular or heart-shaped. Fig. 12 shows a typical example.

24

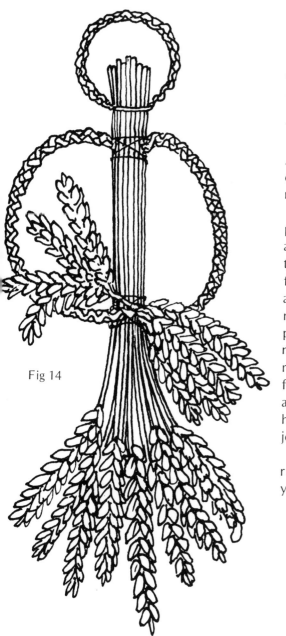

Fig 14

A simple intertwined braid can be made into a 'harvest knot' in trefoil shape, like an ace of clubs, and for the determinedly practical it is perhaps worth mentioning that circular table mats can be made by winding braid up like a snail's shell or a tape measure and sewing into place.

Traditional Maiden

A small well-matched bunch of straws, tied together and decorated with two lengths of four-straw plait or seven-straw round plait, makes the simplest symbolic maiden.

Tie the tail ends of the two plaits together, and arch the plaits over so that the ears hang downwards (fig. 13). Divide about twenty matched straws into two equal bunches, and with the ears downwards attach one bunch behind and the other in front of the joined plaits (fig. 14). Make a tight join with thread above and below the plait. The plaits form the 'arms' of the maiden, and the bundle of straws the body. The ends of the plaits with their ears should be tied across the front of the maiden as shown in the figure, arranging the ears if possible in a rhythmic curve. The ends of the stalks of the central bundle form the 'head' of the maiden, and should be trimmed neatly to a tidy shape. A 'halo' of four-straw plait can be added about the head as indicated in the figure, and ribbons can be tied at the joins in plain red, blue, green or gold.

Indeed, further braids can be added anywhere. There is no rule or law which governs the design, only a tradition to guide you.

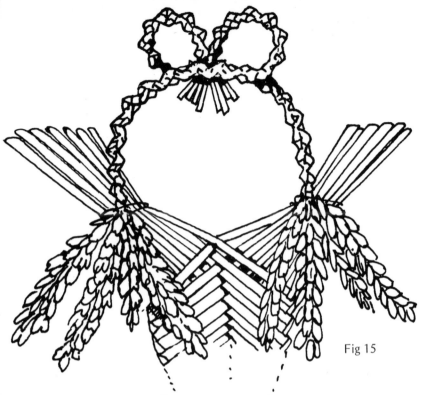

Fig 15

4 Welsh Fans

A whole array of dollies comes together under the title of Welsh fans. They are instantly recognizable, for they are all flat in cross-section and fringed with corn ears like bearded faces. Just as beards vary in style and trim, each with its own character, so Welsh fans have differing personalities according to their shape and, most particularly, the quality of the corn heads themselves. The technique for making them is always the same, however, and the common factor of flatness, like the fernleaf which may have been their inspiration, makes them eminently practical as wall hangings.

As well as being decorative, fans are extremely good practice for the beginner. Workers who have tried the four-straw plait

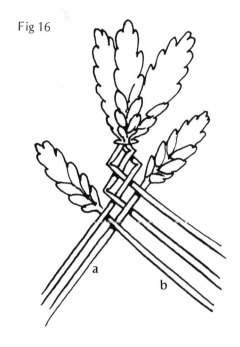

Fig 16

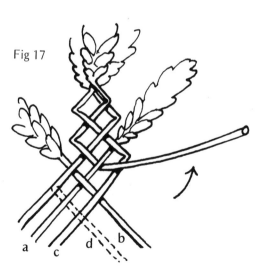

Fig 17

will have discovered the mangling effect of clutching the straw with the whole hand. A plait will not be ruined in this way, but a more ambitious form certainly will, and it is important to remember that straws should be held in the fingertips at the point where a fold or bend is to be made, but nowhere else. Each straw is bent only a few times when making a Welsh fan, and the beginner will be pleased to find that work proceeds rapidly.

Welsh Border Fan

Select twenty-five well-matched straws and tie three together close to the ear. Plait these together, left over centre, right over centre, left over centre. Then stop, keeping two straws on one side, one on the other. The next two straws are now inserted.

Fig. 16 shows how this should be done. Place the first new straw *under* the straw on the right to lie at **a**. Place the second new ear under the straw on the left to lie at **b**. There are now three straws to the right, two to the left, and they must be locked in position.

Holding the straws between the first and second fingers of the left hand, raise the centre straw of the two on the right with the left thumb (fig. 17). Then with the right hand bend the outer straw on the right-hand side down to lie at **c**. Similarly, the centre straw at **a** should now be raised and the outer straw on the left folded under it to lie at **d**. The new straws are now locked in place. Repeat this fold once on each side, and you are ready to insert the next pair of straws. This is done as before. The straw goes *under* the outer straw, but lies on top of the others in its path. It is not plaited through them. New straws are never added singly, always in pairs, one straw to each side. Two locking folds are made on each side after the new straws are added, and in this way the design grows in both length and width until all the new straws have been incorporated.

Six or seven locking folds are now made on each side, and what is left of the straw is gathered together on each side, where it is tied tightly in a bunch. The projecting ends of the straws are now trimmed level.

The Welsh fan is usually hung with the corn ears pointing downwards, and a decorative hanger can be made with a length of four-straw plait. If two lengths of four-straw plait, each with a bunch of ears, is used the ears will cover the attachment point, and the free ends can be shaped into a bow and tied securely (fig. 15).

The Long Fan

Inevitably the fan gets wider as new ears are added, unless some of the straws are cut out as work progresses. By cutting out as many straws as are introduced, the width of the fan's spine is kept constant, and in this way the Welsh long fan is produced. This is how it is done.

1. After fifteen straws have been used, and one locking fold made on each side, cut off the straw which is third from the centre on each side, as shown in fig. 19.
2. Make one more locking fold on each side, and introduce two more straws.
3. Make one more locking fold on each side, and again cut away the straws which lie third from the centre on each side.
4. Continue in this way until all the new straws have been introduced.
5. Continue making locking folds, but cut away the third straw from the centre on each side after each pair of locking folds until only five straws remain.
6. Plait these straws as a five-straw plait until it is long enough to be turned back on itself as a handle (fig. 18). The plait can be fastened with thread or a ribbon, and the ends trimmed.

The sharp ends of the cut straws protrude from the back, and can be tucked into the body of the fan without showing on the front. The dolly is now ready to hang up.

Long fans can, in theory, be any length, though it is not

Fig 18

Fig 19. The width of the long fan is kept constant by cutting off as many straws as you add.

practical to make them too much like centipedes, as they become more and more floppy as they grow.

The ear of the straw is well displayed in this dolly, which is why it is important to choose straws which match. Barley, with its handsome whiskery ears, can be used to make long fans, though the straw is short and fine and it is not an easy material for the beginner. Its ear repeats in miniature the shape of the whole, but as barley has a wide head compared to that of wheat you will need to make three or four locking folds (instead of two) before inserting each new straw.

Fig 20. The Neck

5 Spirals with a Core

Fig 21

Joining straws

Cut the ear from the top of a straw. Because straws taper slightly towards the top, there is no difficulty in inserting the tapered end into the butt of another straw. One cannot go on for ever plaiting straw without encountering the need to make such joins, as shown in fig. 21. They are easy to make, especially if the thinner straw is trimmed on the bias, like a quill. They are best concealed if they come near or under a fold in the plaiting, and you will soon learn always to make joins at a corner so that they are inconspicuous.

The solid spiral

A spiral is the natural result of a simple sequence of plaiting. It has the double virtue of being both spectacular to look at and almost automatic to make. It is the technique most commonly used for the symbolic 'neck' and spiral dollies have been made for centuries in every corn-growing country in Europe from east to west, and north to south. Every beginner in strawcraft must

Far left The Long Fan

31

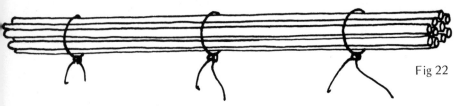

Fig 22

have this technique under his belt before calling himself a dolly-maker.

1. To make the core, prepare a bundle of corn, without ears. Tie about ten straws together several times along their length (fig. 22). 'Reject' straws will do for this, as they will not be seen in the finished dolly.

2. Tie five more straws under the ears, and around one end of the core, spreading them so that they stick out like the spokes of an umbrella. Seen from above, straws **b, c, d,** and **e** should be at right angles to one another, and straw **a** should be alongside **b** (fig. 23).

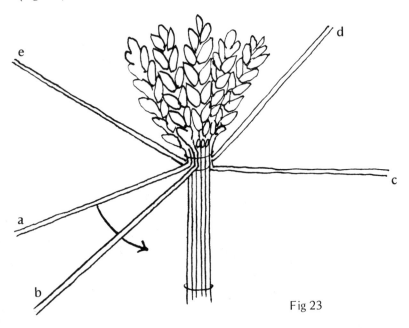

Fig 23

Plate 1 The Suffolk Basket

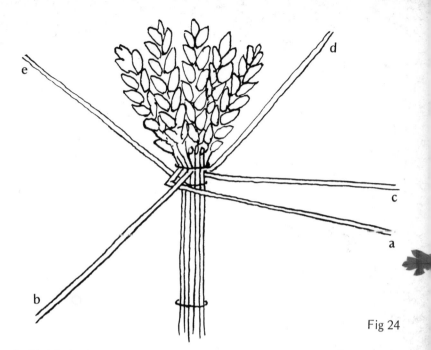

Fig 24

3. Hold the core in the left hand and with the right hand bring straw **a** under **b** to lie below **c** (fig. 24).
4. Give the bundle a quarter turn clockwise so that straws **a** and **c** lie in the position previously occupied by **a** and **b**.
5. Bring straw **c** under **a** and across to lie by **d**.
6. Again make a quarter turn and bring **d** across to **e**.
7. Continue working down the core, joining straws as necessary.

It is a delight to see the spiral form emerging without effort. Avoid if possible making several joins in close sequence, as this will weaken the structure. You can hide the join under the fold by cutting the straw just where it will be covered by the fold in **a**, as shown in fig. 25, but insert the new straw before folding the neighbouring straw over. You should push the new straw into the butt until it reaches the previous angle. If the butt end should split, straw **a** will hold them both in place.

It is infuriating sometimes to find that, with the work well under way, there are no new straws left with a diameter small

Plate 2 Harvest Nells

35

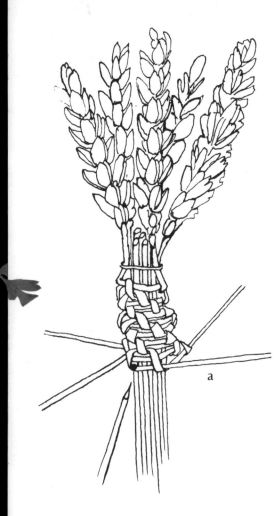

Fig 25. Hiding a join

enough to fit inside the butt. Rather than abandon the work, a join can be made by fitting the new straw *behind* the old one, and allowing the cover fold to bind them both in tightly. The old butt can then be trimmed off near the fold.

You must make the plaits as tightly as possible, to keep the work even and strong. The core can be 'padded' at its centre by binding in extra, short, straws, so that the form swells in the middle like a cigar. When the end of the cigar is reached the dolly is completed by tying all the straws tightly together and trimming off, or by cutting the working straws short, and pushing each one down between the spiral and the core. The core can then be trimmed flush with the plaiting. If you wish to continue the plaiting beyond the end of the core, cut off one of the working straws, and with the rest plait a length of four-straw plait to fold over as a crook or hanger.

Indeed, there are countless ways of embellishing and beribboning the traditional baton-like neck, and the inventive straw-worker will soon think of original forms of his own.

A Neck with two heads

This nicely balanced variant has ears at both ends, and can be made as follows.

1. Tie together twelve small straws about 14 inches long, with ears left on, to make a core, and attach a further five without ears for plaiting.
2. Work 1½ inches of spiral, and then add three long straws to the core by their butts, so that the ears extend a few inches beyond the length of the core.
3. Work another 1½ inches and add to the core another three straws a little shorter in length, so that their ears line up with the previous batch.
4. Repeat this for a further two sections, each of about 1½ inches, so that your spiral is about 6 inches long, and there are twelve level ears of corn at the lower end of the core.

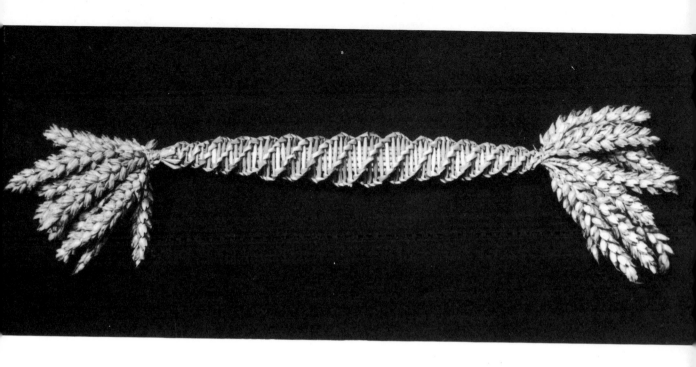

Above A neck with two heads

5. Continue for a further 2 inches, and then cut away three of the original straws in the core flush with the plaiting.
6. Repeat this after another 1½ inches of spiral, and again after each 1½ inches until all the original straws have been cut away, and the core consists of the twelve straws with ears.
7. The final short length of spiral should be plaited and the end tied and trimmed off near the ears so that the dolly is a symmetrical shape.

This shape is often hung horizontally with a length of three-straw plait as a ribbon. It is shown above.

The Harvest Cross

One of the most appropriate symbols to make with the baton-like cored spiral is the cross, and after the Church in the mid-nineteenth century admitted harvest celebrations as an

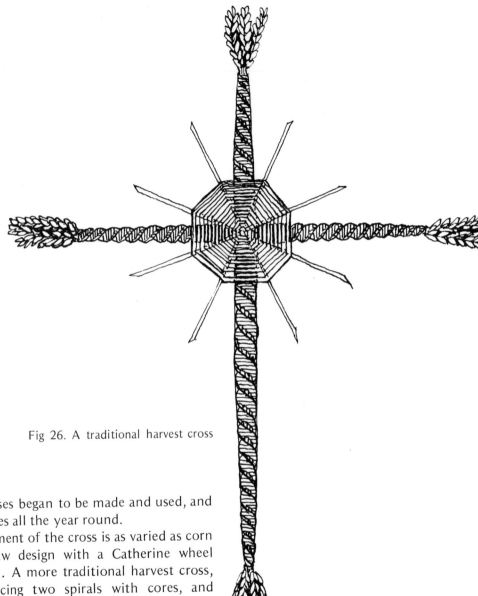

Fig 26. A traditional harvest cross

official festival, harvest crosses began to be made and used, and some of them stay in churches all the year round.

The decoration and ornament of the cross is as varied as corn itself, and an unusual straw design with a Catherine wheel centre is shown on page 41. A more traditional harvest cross, however, is made by splicing two spirals with cores, and decorating the intersections. The arms of the cross can be made to any size, by introducing new straws into the core as the ends of the original ones are reached or simply by using other materials such as canes. For really large crosses, wires or canes are essential in the cores to give rigidity.

Having bound two cores of appropriate length for the shaft and the cross piece, with ears at the extremities, a harvest cross is made as follows:

1. Mark on the cores with pencil or with a temporary tie of ribbon the position for the intersection, and work a spiral plait around each core up to ½ inch before the mark.
2. Tie the working straw and its neighbour together temporarily with cotton to prevent unravelling.
3. Tightly bind with thread the *core* of the longer arm at the point where the plaiting stops (**a**).
4. Separate the core straws of the longer arm below this tie into two equal parts and between them insert the other core up to the point of intersection, and hard up against the tie (**a**). Make sure that not only the core but the plaiting straws as well are spliced through the main shaft (**b**), and that they come out regularly on the other side.
5. Tie the core of the shaft firmly underneath the cross piece to hold it in place.
6. Bring the plaiting straws of the shaft over the cross piece as shown in fig. 27, and continue plaiting the spiral down the shaft until it is complete.

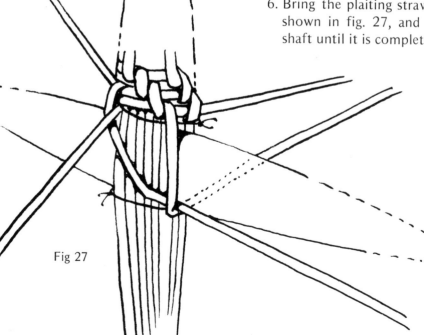

Fig 27

7. Return to the cross piece, complete the spiral, tie in the ends.

The plaiting straws should be tied down and trimmed off neatly when they reach the ears at the end of the cores. Decorative bosses or bindings made from flattened and glued strips of straw can be made for the end of the arms in place of the ears if you wish, though the full heads of corn seem particularly appropriate to celebrate harvest festival.

The intersection of the cross can be covered with a star or medallion (see Chapter 9) and this gives a fine opportunity for ingenuity in design. If the medallion is to be a flat one, then a simple spiders-web weave is appropriate, and this is described on page 87.

Right The Catherine-wheel centre of a harvest cross made by George Dabinett.

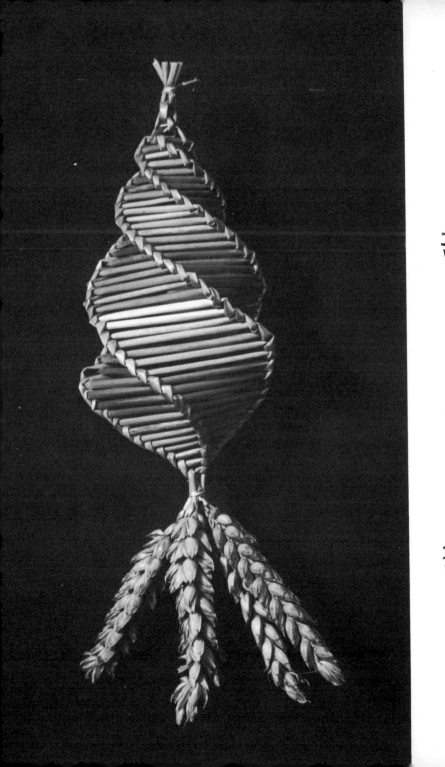

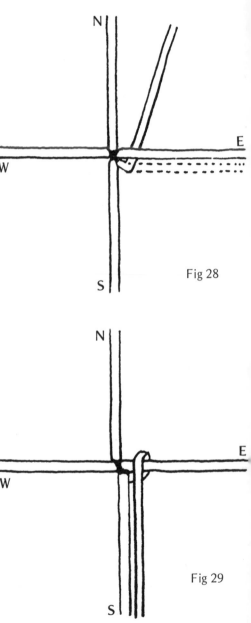

Left The Yorkshire Spiral

Fig 28

Fig 29

6 Hollow Spirals

A spiral plaited tightly around a core will take the shape of whatever it is surrounding. If you make a spiral plait which is hollow, you must control the shape yourself by careful placing of the straws at the folds.

Many beginners find the jump from the solid to the hollow spiral a daunting one, but the technique is very simple. Instead of working *down* the core, with ears at the top, a hollow spiral is plaited *upwards*, with the ears hanging down and the spiral climbing towards you.

The Basic Spiral

1. Tie five straws together close to the ears and hold them between the first and second fingers of the left hand, ears down.
2. With the thumb of the left hand fold the straws down into a horizontal plane, like the points of the compass, N,S,W and two straws at E fig. 28.
3. With the right hand take the straw at E^1 under E^2, up into a vertical position, and down to lie alongside S, as in fig. 29.
4. Turn the straws in the left hand a quarter of a circle *anti-clockwise*, so that S and E^1 are now pointing east, and take S under E^2, up to vertical and down to lie alongside W.
5. Repeat the quarter turn, and the movements, so that W lies alongside N.

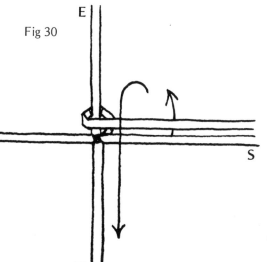

Fig 30

6. Continue taking the lower straw pointing east under its neighbour, up to vertical and down to point south.

If you look down the spiral from above, you will see that a small square pattern is emerging, and you will need to make perhaps two full turns (i.e. eight folds) before this is clearly established.

A little practice will accomplish more than words can. As soon as you have grasped the principle of the active straw going *under its neighbour, up to vertical, and then down towards you* whilst making a quarter turn with the left hand, your spiral will form itself, and grow rapidly.

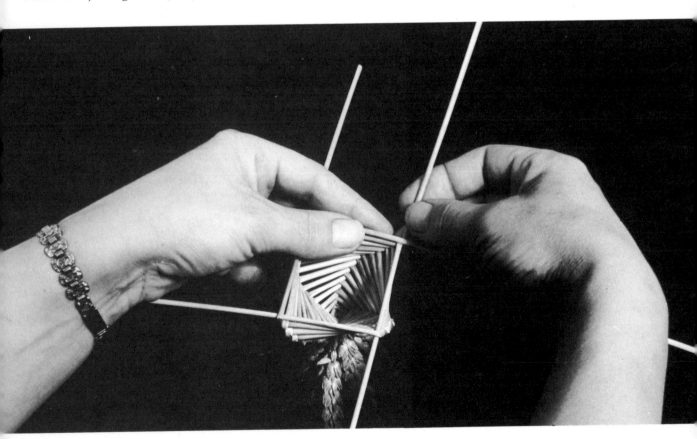

Left and right Neat joins make good spirals.

Direction of Spiral

What happens if instead of bringing the active straw from vertical towards you, you bend it away from you (towards north) and make a clockwise quarter turn instead? The direction of the spiral will be reversed. The principle is the same, and the result will look the same. If this method comes more easily to you, use it. Try reversing the direction when the straws are half used up. You will see the spiral change direction and you may like to use the change to decorative effect.

Left-handers

Left-handed beginners may find it more comfortable to use their right hand to hold the ears, and move the straws with their left hand. The result is the same. You can even change hands as the work proceeds if you wish. This is not exhibitionism — just common sense if one hand becomes tired.

So many variables producing the same result show the folly of insisting on one method. Each straw-worker must use the *direction* which suits him best. He must remember the following golden rules to precision and shape.

1. It is the thumbs which control the precision of the form. The left thumb holds tight the previous joint whilst the right thumb makes the new one. As the quarter turn is made, the left thumb comes down to hold the work in place. It is equally important to make sure that the working straw passes through the vertical position on its way towards making the next joint. This will make the right crease in the straw and a regular firm joint.

2. The final position of the active straw controls the width of the spiral (fig. 31). If you place the active straw at E^2 alongside but *outside* the straw at S, this is going to make the spiral grow in cross-section. *Only* if the active straw is placed immediately on top of straw S will the size remain constant. If the active straw is placed *inside* the straw S the spiral will shrink again in size.

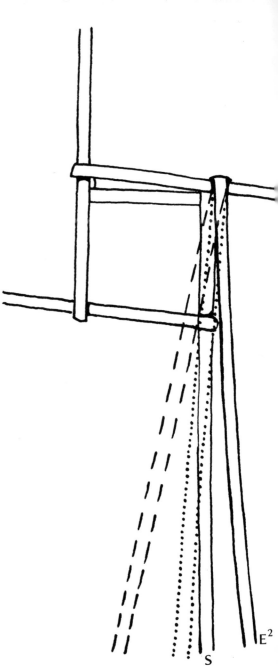

It is natural at the beginning of a spiral to allow the width to grow — indeed it is essential, for at the start the infant spiral has a negligible cross-section. It also comes naturally as the work proceeds to restrict the width again so that the most natural form for the beginner to make is the 'tear-drop' shape of the Yorkshire spiral (page 42). As the spiral comes together again the straws should be bound tightly, and the remaining lengths cut off. If one straw is cut off, the rest can be plaited into a length of four-straw plait (see Chapter 3) to make a hanger.

The Number of Sides to a Spiral

The beginner who has progressed so far is now able to make a spiral and to control its diameter. It is very difficult, when looking at a spiral corn dolly, to *see* how many sides or faces it has. The straw-worker will know it has four sides (for the section he sees as work proceeds is square), and there is always one side less than the number of straws employed. Thus one can make a six-sided spiral with seven straws, though the result may be no more satisfying aesthetically than the basic form already described. The technique is the same but the greater the number of straws, the greater the number of joins per revolution. This is appropriate for some forms described later in this chapter, especially those which represent people or flowers.

The Hereford Lantern or Pyramid

The lantern shape is made in several English counties, as well as countries as far afield as Roumania and Greece. It is a very popular form using the basic spiral plait, and it depends on one additional technique — the reversion of the direction of plaiting.

The best way to learn the technique is to follow the instructions for making the dolly.

1. Take five straws with well-matched ears and plait about 1 inch of narrow spiral.

Fig 31. If you place straw E^2 alongside but outside straw S the spiral will grow. If you put the active straw (shown dotted) directly on top of S the spiral will remain the same size. If you put the active straw (shown dashed) inside straw S the spiral will shrink.

2. Turn the work over so that the ears point upwards and begin plaiting again from this side, starting where the two straws lie together, and using the usual techniques. The new spiral form should be made to widen out by placing the active straws in the E^2 position of fig. 31. Continue working until the level of the plaiting has reached the level of the base of the ears. The sides of the square may now be at least 2 inches long.

3. Now turn the work over again, so that the ears hang down, and start to plait upwards using the same technique. Once again direction will have changed, and your work will have a cross-section as shown below.

4. Allow the spiral to grow in diameter for the first inch or so, and then progressively reduce the width until the form comes together at the top.

5. Tie off the top, or finish with a small plait as a hanger, as shown in fig. 32.

Making a dolly of this kind is an opportunity to show virtuosity, and skill in controlling the shape. The dolly in fig. 32 is often called a 'pyramid' to distinguish it from a 'lantern' which has a second bulge before it is finished at the top, like a tower in the Kremlin. The Norfolk Lantern has yet another and larger bulge at the top, and often these designs are ornamented with miniature spirals or lanterns tied to and hanging from the corners of the 'bell'.

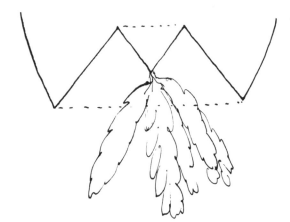

Fig 32. The lantern, with cross section at left showing the structure near the base.

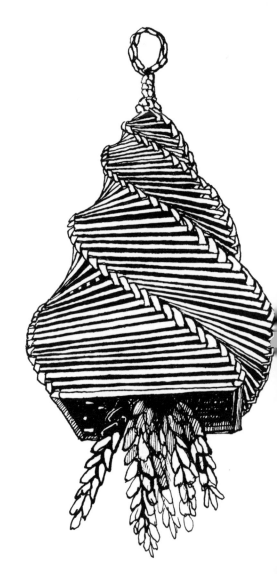

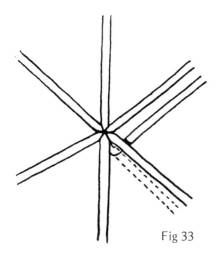

Fig 33

The Suffolk Basket

The greater the number of straws in the plaiting, the more closely will the cross-section of the spiral resemble a circle, and this is useful for such forms as bells. A simple seven-straw spiral dolly on which the beginner can practise is the Suffolk basket, shown in Plate 1, page 33, and described below.

1. Tie seven straws with good ears together and spread them equally as in fig. 33.
2. Plait the straws as for a five-straw spiral plait but make sure that the radiating pattern of the straws has six corners. The work is moved through one-sixth of a circle, not a quarter turn, each time a fold is made — there are six folds per revolution.
3. Allow the work to widen until a cone of pleasing proportion is made.
4. Tie together the working straw and its neighbour close to the joint, using a thread of unobtrusive colour.

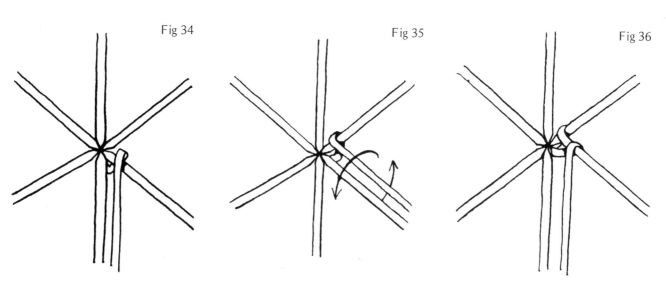

Fig 34   Fig 35   Fig 36

Figs 33-36 show how a seven-straw plait is begun.

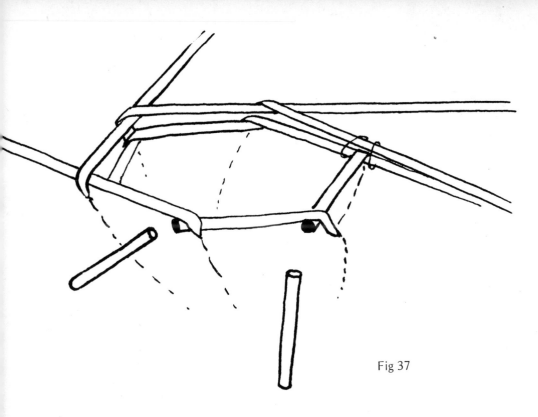

Fig 37

5. Trim off the ends of all the straws close to the folds (preferably when the straw has dried out completely), fig. 37.
6. Make three braids of three-straw plait, and attach them to three of the six corners with thread. These braids should be tied together at a length of about six inches from the basket or joined to a plaited ring which can act as a hanger.

The Suffolk basket can act as an attractive wall holder for dried flowers, but the individual lengths of the braids — which can be attached to all the six corners if you prefer — are critical. They control the angle at which the basket will hang from the wall, and it is helpful if they can be adjusted individually. A variation of this design, made from withies, can be closed over at the top and used as a rattle, provided that something that rattles (like a handful of beans) is put inside before the shape is closed up.

The Corn Lily

Combined with heads of corn, barley and oats, plaited straw bells can make attractive additions to floral displays. You can probably think of several flowers which can appropriately be made of straw and instructions are given here for a basic lily.

1. Make a 'stalk' by threading a piece of florists' wire through one straw without an ear, and add seven straws with ears. Tie them together under the ears and hook the wired straw over at the tie so that it cannot escape from the bundle.
2. Hold the bundle with the ears *upwards,* and the wired straw pointing downwards between the first and second fingers of the left hand. Begin a seven-straw spiral plait so that it encloses the ears (figs 38 and 39).
3. Widen the spiral rapidly and when the bell of the flower is an appropriate size tie the working straw to its neighbour, as for the Suffolk basket.
4. Cut off the projecting parts of the straws close to the folds.
5. The wired straw can now be bent to a life-like angle, as shown on page 53.

Corn heads can be used to represent 'leaves' in association with these 'flowers', and it is perhaps wise not to bend the stem straws until all flowers are ready to be put in the arrangement, when the group will suggest the most elegant angle for the flower heads.

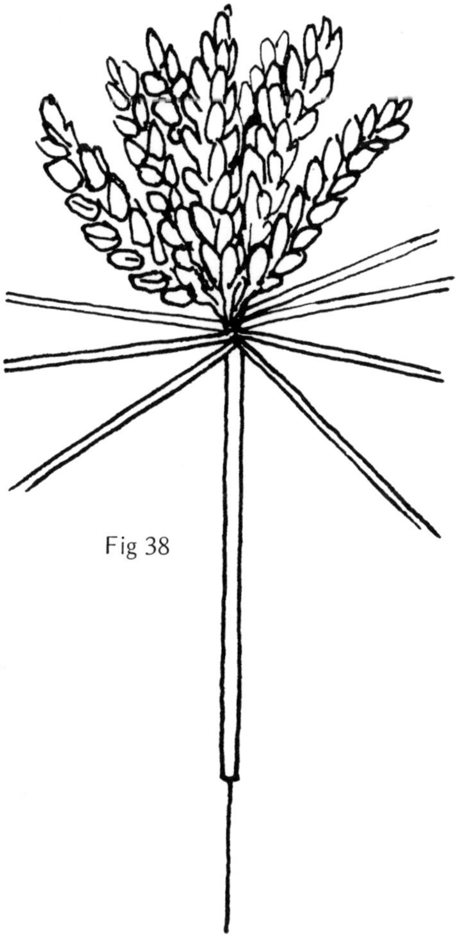

Fig 38

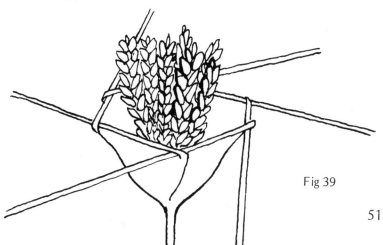

Fig 39

The Cornucopia

One of the most persistent features of ornamental decoration is the horn of plenty, a popular symbol of harvest abundance with goods of all kinds spilling out of its mouth. It is, of course, the most unsuitably-shaped receptacle for large quantities of anything, as any child disappointed by an ice cream cornet knows, but its wide mouth gives the right impression, and flower arrangers love it.

It is such an ideal shape for straw-workers that one might be excused for imagining that the corn dolly maker had invented it. Any spiral is a potential cornucopia, just as any little snail is potentially a large snail, though the really large shape should be made from seven or nine-straw plait, so that the individual facets of the mouth of the horn are not too long. The instructions are simple.

1. Plait as for the Suffolk basket, but increase the cross-section slowly.
2. Pay special attention to the corners, for some strain is put on these in the shaping.
3. The mouth of the horn should widen at an ever increasing rate — a 'growth' curve — but the axis of the horn should remain straight, so that it has the appearance of a tall cone. When the cone has reached the desired length, tie up the working straw and cut off the remaining lengths as for the Suffolk basket.
4. Curve the horn in the hands until it has reached the desired shape, and tie a string from the mouth to the apex tightly, while it dries. When dry, the horn will keep this shape, and the string can be removed.
5. Tie a bundle of ears of the same or varying kinds together, and arrange them inside, but spilling out of the mouth. A horn of plenty normally rests on its side.

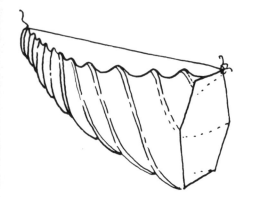

Fig 40. The horn is bent into a curve by tying the tip to the mouth with string while the corn dries.

Opposite Top left: the Corn Lily; top right: the Harvest Basket; below: the Cornucopia

52

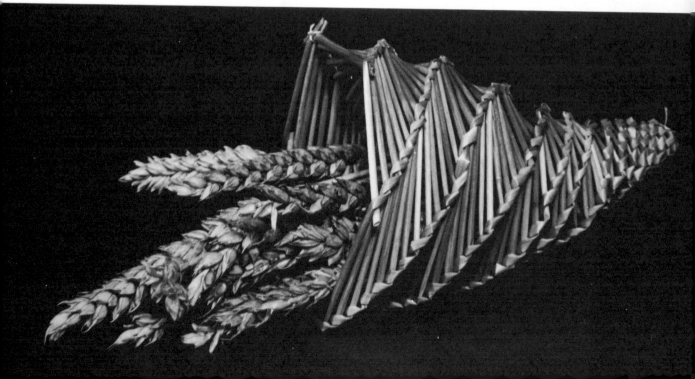

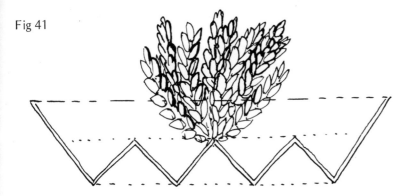

Fig 41

The Harvest Basket

A basket from plaited straw will be too fragile for any practical use, but it can be used as a decorative item or an attractive harvest symbol.

1. Tie together nine straws close to the ears and work a short section of spiral plait — about four rounds.
2. Turn the work over and, with the ears facing upwards as for the Hereford lantern, work another four rounds, increasing the diameter rapidly.
3. Reverse the work again, and with the ears hanging down make another four rounds, again increasing the diameter rapidly, so that the work has the cross-section shown above.
4. Once more reverse the work, and plait upwards the 'sides' of the basket.
5. Finish off the rim of the basket as for the Suffolk basket when the sides are of a happy height, and spread the ears so that they appear to fill the basket.
6. Make a bundle of four-straw plait, or seven-straw round plait according to the size of the basket; arch over the handle, and join at both ends.

A smaller version can be made by omitting stages 3 and 4, and working more rounds of stage 2 for the sides of the basket, as shown in the picture on page 53.

Harvest Nell

When you have thoroughly mastered the technique of widening and narrowing the spiral plait you can use it for lots of forms. Undoubtedly some of the early corn dollies used for harvest customs were made into human form, and I have no doubt that some of them were made from spiral plaits. With this tradition in mind I made Harvest Nell (see Plate 2), a buxom country woman holding a miniature sheaf of corn. This is how to make her.

1. Tie nine straws under the ears; the ears are going to make the top knot.
2. Plait a small spherical spiral for the head, but take care not to close it up too tightly.
3. Continue working for two or three rounds without changing the diameter, to form the neck.
4. Increase the diameter sharply for the shoulders and bust, reduce the diameter again for the waist, and finish the body form with a wide bell-like skirt, tying in the working straw and cutting off all the ends as for the Suffolk basket.
5. To make the arms take two groups each of five straws, without ears, and push them through the body near the shoulders as shown in fig. 42, five straws in each direction. Bind both bunches tightly as shown. The ends of each side will be covered by the plaiting of the opposite arm.
6. Work each arm into a five-straw spiral, narrowing the width towards the wrists, tying the straws together and cutting the ends a short distance beyond the tie to form the hands. Billowing mutton-chop sleeves can be made, but you must take care not to allow the sleeve spirals to become too large, or they are difficult to fold round to the front.
7. Form a small 'sheaf' of corn with six or seven ears, and short stalks. Fold the hands close together and bind them and the sheaf with thread.
8. After the plaiting is finished, and while the corn is still damp, fold the ears down over the back of the head and secure them

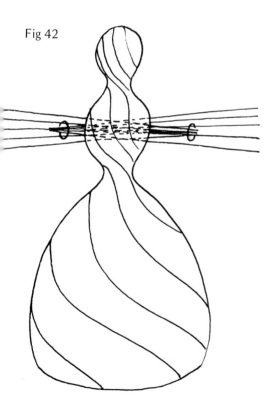

Fig 42

by binding them to the head with thread. When the corn is thoroughly dry, remove the thread, and the 'hair' will stay in place.

It is extraordinary how the Harvest Nell will assert her personality in the making. She soon assumes a definite character as minor details in the plaiting give clues and the finishing touch to her manner will be given by the angle at which she holds the sheaf of corn. Place several Harvest Nells together and they seem to be having a conversation.

The Cambridgeshire Handbell

A nine-straw spiral plait is used for the handbell, unless it is particularly small, in which case a seven-straw plait is sufficient. To make the shape, a core is necessary for the handle but not for the bell.

1. Choose nine straws and tie them at the ears. The ears will form the clapper of the bell, and the next part of the straws will form the core of the handle. You must judge the length required for this, and tie the straws again at the top of the handle.
2. Spread out the nine straws over this tie and work a tight spiral plait back down over the core.
3. When the end of the handle has been reached, change the technique for that of the spiral without a core, holding the handle downwards, and work an expanding spiral into a bell shape.
4. Tie the active straw to its neighbour, and when the dolly is dry trim off the projecting ends.
5. Finish the shape with a ribbon tied round the junction of the handle with the bell.

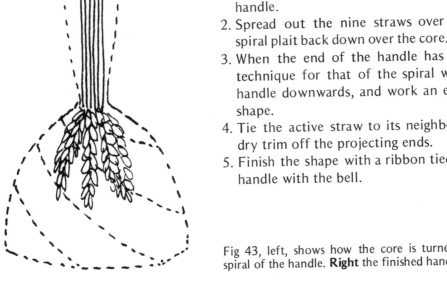

Fig 43, left, shows how the core is turned over at the top to make the spiral of the handle. **Right** the finished handbell

The Yorkshire Candlestick

This form depends on a crisp division between handle, bowl and holder, and is not an easy one to make.

1. Take a core of about ten straws without ears and tie five straws with ears to the end of the core. The ears represent the flame and the five working straws should be plaited down the core in a tight spiral.
2. When the end of the candle is reached, add seven more straws to the core, pointing up the candle. Tie these, the five working straws and the core tightly together.
3. Bend the seven new straws out at right angles to the core, and work a core-less spiral out from the centre, enlarging the shape rapidly to make a shallow bowl. When the bowl is wide enough, attach the active straw to its neighbour, and trim off the ends.
4. Now return to the five working straws from the spiral of the candle. Add two more working straws by pushing them into the core, one on each side, and continue down the stem of the candle in seven-straw spiral plait.
5. When the base of the candle is reached, work the base as a wide spreading core-less spiral plait, finishing as with the Suffolk basket, and trimming the core level with the base.

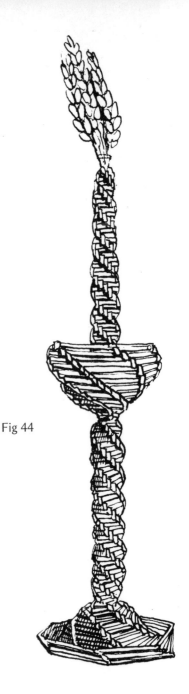

Fig 44

Right Mother Earth, a spiral dolly designed by Mrs M. Lambeth.

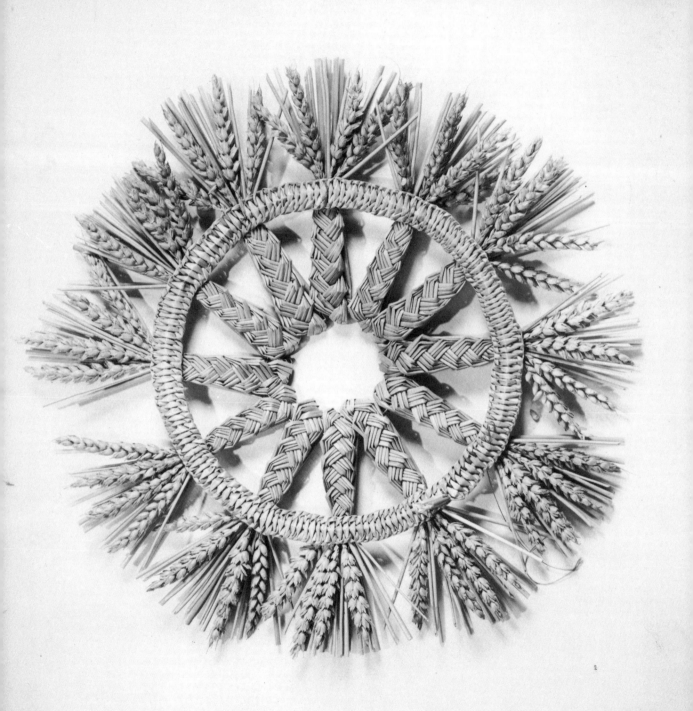

7 Combined Techniques

Spiral and braided plaits woven into traditional symbolic forms, and described in the preceding chapters, provide enough variety for many straw-workers, whilst others want to experiment and make abstract or representational shapes which, as far as we know, have never been part of a harvest ceremony. A spirit of invention is shown by such groups as Somerset House, Cheddar, which has produced the original design shown opposite, called the Wedmore Wheel, as well as complex mobile spirals in which pyramids without cores hang one inside the other, free to turn in a current of air.

In choosing subjects for experimental designs it is worth remembering that complicated objects like cars, or houses which have flat planes, do not lend themselves to imitation in straw, whilst organic and natural forms, provided they are simple, are often good subjects. I have myself seen straw creatures ranging from sea-horses to cockerels, and can imagine many others such as squirrels or lobsters which would make quite spectacular designs. All the plaiter needs is a reference photograph and a good technique.

The instructions which follow are for eight simple subjects which involve plaiting for at least part of the design. Non-plaited animals and straw designs are found in Chapters 8 and 9.

Left The Wedmore Wheel

The Horseshoe

It is not surprising that this traditional good-luck symbol has been borrowed by straw-workers for it is both simple to make and an effective decoration.

Make a core about 12 inches long, and over this plait a five-straw spiral. The five weaving straws, which should be without ears, can be pushed into the end of the core, bound and turned back on themselves to make a neat beginning to the plait, and they can similarly be tucked back into the core on finishing over the opposite end. Whilst the plait is still damp, it should be curved gently into a horseshoe shape, and the two ends tied together with string so that the horseshoe holds its shape while it dries. If it is shaped around a jam-jar its curve will be a regular one.

It is usual to hang a horseshoe with its opening facing upwards, and a hanger can be made of ribbon, or of thin plait with corn ears for decoration where it joins the main spiral.

A straw horseshoe is by tradition a Suffolk dolly. It can also be an attractive addition to the decorations for a wedding.

Fig 45

A Decorative Circle

Many objects which are hung on walls are enhanced by some kind of frame. Since the spiral plait can be adapted to any generous curved shape, it can be made to surround a pair of dollies, as illustrated in Plate 3, page 67.

Make a 3 foot length of five-straw spiral plait around a core and shape it into a circle or an oval while it is still damp. Bind the two ends together tightly with thread, and add at the same point a second smaller spiral bent into a loop to make a 'handle', covering the join with a group of ears or a ribbon.

From this same join you can hang a Yorkshire spiral, a pair of pyramids or Hereford lanterns so that they hang centrally within the surround. You may be surprised to find how small your dolly has to be to fit completely within its frame.

The Chandelier

Popular and much-plaited is the straw-work 'chandelier' which gives the straw-dolly maker the opportunity to display many designs in one pendant feature.

To make a chandelier of moderate size you will need to make a circle out of five-straw spiral plait around a core 4 or 5 feet long. To give the core strength bind a stout wire in with the straws, projecting several inches beyond the core at each end. When the spiral plaiting is complete bend it into an even circle, and push the protruding wires into the cores as shown in fig. 46. Where the spiral ends butt against each other, tie together firmly with thread, and glue if necessary. Several lengths of four-straw plait should be tied to this circle of straw at regular intervals to form suspenders, gathered together at the centre, where a small spiral boss can be added to emphasize the join. A strong plait — perhaps a seven-straw round plait — must be made from the central suspension point, and it is important to be able to adjust the lengths of the four-straw plaits to ensure that the circle is horizontal.

Fig 46

Fig 47. The Chandelier

Three, four or more dollies, such as Hereford lanterns, can be hung from the circle, and a large spiral form from the centre. Place these pendants symmetrically round the circle, and intersperse them if you wish with straw stars.

Really elaborate and large chandeliers can be made with more than one circle, and radiating spokes for strength as in the wagon wheel. Remember that if you start to make a chandelier you will need to prepare a great deal of straw.

A Flattened Spiral

A flattened spiral is an uninspiring name for a fascinating design which has the quality of an optical illusion. Unlike other spirals, the flat spiral lacks rigidity, and it needs very great care in the making.

Using nine straws, with the ears left on, make a conventional spiral, but reverse the direction every five rounds. The diameter will grow rapidly, and the structure will become floppy if it exceeds about 12 inches diameter, so it should be finished off by turning in the working straw and cutting off the ends when it has reached this size. The photograph below illustrates the finished result. The flattened spiral can be hung on a wall like a plate if a length of four-straw plait is made into a loop and tied to the centre at the back. If it is hung horizontally like the chandelier, additional spirals or plaits can be suspended from the perimeter and ridges.

Right A Flattened Spiral

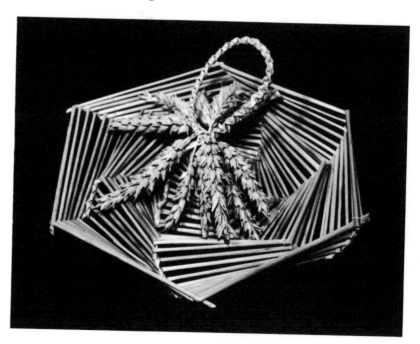

The Wagon Wheel

A straw wheel with radiating spokes can be made from a circle plaited as for the chandelier. If the circumference of the circle is 3 feet, you will need to make 'spokes' 11 inches long and three of these made of seven-straw round plait need to be strengthened by threading a flower wire about 15 inches long down the central straw of the plait. The straws must be tied tightly with thread at each end of the plait to prevent unravelling, and the three plaits should be arranged as a six-pointed star, and tightly bound at their centres, as shown in fig. 48. This central join is less bulky if the straws in the centre section of each plait can be left straight and unplaited for about one inch. At the hub, to

Fig 48

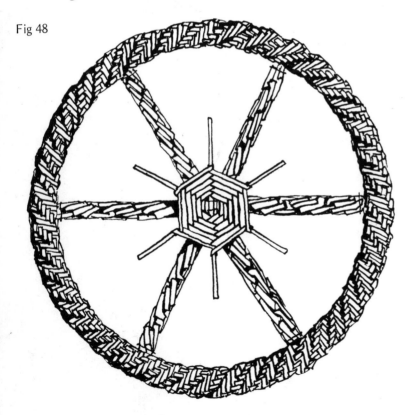

Plate 3 A Decorative Circle

cover the central join, a boss made from seven or nine-straw spiral can be added, or a spider's web medallion, as described in Chapter 9.

The spokes can now be added to the rim by working the protruding wires into the straw of the circle. Care must be taken not to split straws with the wires, and thread ties should be added to prevent the spokes from working loose.

Tree of Oats

A tree made from oats is an ambitious piece of work and its success depends upon the shape and grace of its limbs. The head of an oat straw has more of the look of a branch with leaves than other seed heads, though barley heads can be used for dramatic shapes by straw-workers who can master its difficult nature.

A single straw reinforced with wire down its centre should be used as the core for a four-straw spiral plait made from oats. The spiral should be made in the same way as the five-straw spiral, but its section will be triangular, and its diameter must be kept small. Add more straws of oats to the core as work proceeds by inserting the straw through the spiral plait into the core and allowing its head to protrude from the spiral like a leafy branch.

Work several such plaits, extending from 2 to 4 inches in length. These branches with their twigs and leaves should be combined, as shown in fig. 49, to become boughs and finally the main trunk of the tree. The plaiting straws from one limb should be used to plait down the combined cores, and the plaiting straws from the other limb cut off below the join, though as the trunk becomes thicker some of these straws from the tributary limb can be used in the spiral or added to the main core. By the time the trunk is finished, it has a thick core with a nine or more straw spiral plait around it.

Fig 49

Plate 4 Two corn husk dolls, as described in Chapter 10.

Fig 50. A tree of oats

The particular character of certain trees can be captured effectively in straw if the habit of the branches is carefully studied, and you can twist the trunks into gnarled shapes if you wish.

Although the wires in the core come together to give the tree greater strength as it becomes thicker, it will almost certainly be top heavy and difficult to balance. A heavy base is needed, and this can be made of plaster of Paris or wood with a hole in the centre through which the trunk can disappear so that the straw roots can be firmly anchored on the underside.

Your oat tree need not stand alone. You can use it with a flower arrangement, or in a miniature garden, but take care that it does not get damp for if it does its seeds may sprout, or it may get mildewed.

A Wall Hanging

Many people feel that the best way of displaying corn dollies is within a rigid framework of straw. The circular frame already described gives emphasis and grace to a single shape, but where a whole collection of different shapes is to be displayed a rectangular and symmetrical frame is best. Fig. 51. shows one such arrangement, with a spiral at the top strengthened with stiff wire in its core. The vertical bars should be of five or seven-straw spiral, and where there are intersections medallions or stars can be added to cover the join. A variety of dollies can be hung in the spaces, and ears of corn can be suspended below the bottom bar to provide a fringe of tassels. A frame of this kind can be added to as your collection of dollies for display grows, but it is only likely to remain successful if its final form is symmetrical and its members are stout enough for its finished size. Canvas can be used as an effective backing material.

Fig 51

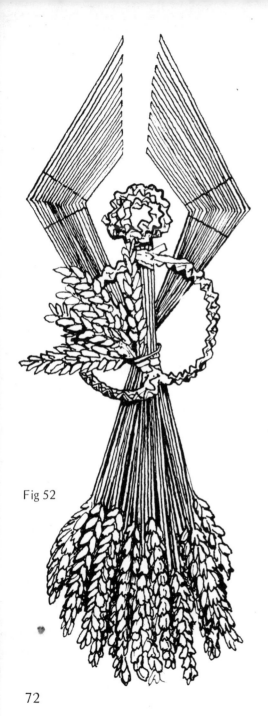

Fig 52

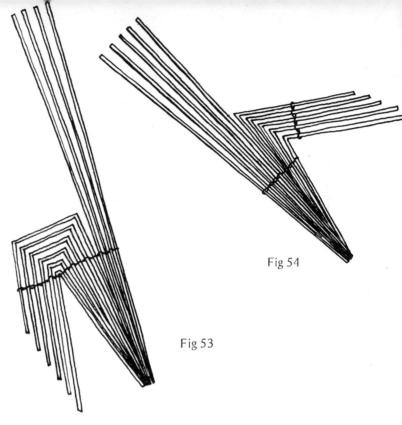

Fig 54

Fig 53

The Angel

As straw dollies become ever more popular as features of church decoration, both at harvest and nativity festivals, it is not surprising that straw angels are popular subjects, and they can be made from plaited or folded straws or combinations of the two.

A bunch of straws with ears forms the body with the ears as the fringe to the dress. From the binding at the waist spring the wings, made from groups of straws, ten on each side, arranged fan-wise and bent downwards or upwards as in figs. 53 and 54. As with the decorative maiden (Chapter 3) the arms holding a sheaf of corn ears are made from four-straw plait, and being an angel the plaited head needs a plaited halo.

Right A selection of dollies made by George Dabinett of Somerset.

George Dabinett
STRAW PLAITER AND
CORN DOLLY MAKER

SOMERSET GUILD OF CRAFTSMEN

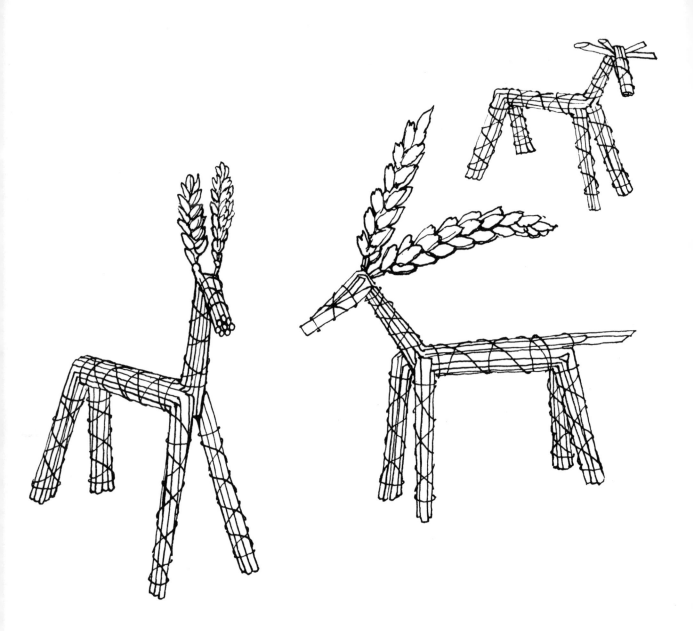

Fig 55. A straw menagerie

8 Straw Animals

Making animals without plaiting is a popular introduction to strawcraft for children, and the results are often in great demand for Christmas and other festive tableaux, as well as attractive table placemarkers for parties.

The menagerie is varied, and the technique for making familiar four-legged animals is very simple. Using the same method, the shape and character of the animal can be varied by altering the proportions of the limbs and neck.

The Quadruped

1. Take 40 straws without ears, at least 12 inches long. Arrange them so that the butt ends are all at one end, and bind together in two places so that the bundle is divided into three roughly equal parts.
2. Start with the rear legs, at the butt end of the bundle. Fold seventeen adjacent straws from one side down to form one leg, and tie these together near the base. Then fold seventeen straws down on the other side to make the other leg, and tie near the foot. This leaves six straws in the centre which will make the tail. Do not make it yet.
3. Make the front legs by folding down thirteen straws on each side and tying near the feet. This will leave fourteen straws to form the neck.

Fig 56. Forming the quadruped and binding the legs and muzzle.

75

4. Make the neck and head by folding the straws first upwards and then, nearer the top, downward. Of course the position of the fold for the head at the top of the neck will govern the length of the neck and the type of animal. Bind the head tightly around the muzzle.

5. Take four short pieces of straw and slip them between the fold at the junction of the head and neck to make the ears and horns. Antlers of various shapes can be made by using ears of wheat, as shown in fig. 58. Alternatively (fig. 57), only two ears of corn are needed, and if you insert one from each side, the corn head will form the antler, and the stub the ear. The angle of the ears will affect the alertness of the animals. Horns can, of course, be made of small spiral plaits. You may wish to trim off the muzzle to an appropriate length.

6. Using a coloured string, bind the animal's body after the fashion of cross gartering, beginning at the join of the neck and body. Leaving a few inches of string loose at the end, make a single tie around the collarbone area, and then a spiral binding along the body and down one hind leg. Make two straight turns at the bottom of the leg and then bind back up, forming the crosses. Without cutting the string, continue down the other back leg, up the leg again and back along the body to the front legs. Bind these up similarly, one after the other, and then work up the neck to the nose, and back to the collar. Tie the string to the original loose end in a light knot or decorative bow. The remainder of the string can be used as reins if you wish.

7. Trim the straws of the feet level, and splay them out slightly so that the animal will stand firmly.

8. Now tackle the tail. Like the angle of the neck it is very important in giving clues to the animal's character. You can leave the six straws sticking straight out, curve them down, fan them out, or curl them upwards. To make a curly tail keep its curl when the straw has dried you may have to tie it temporarily in position.

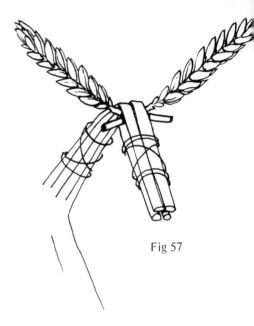

Fig 57

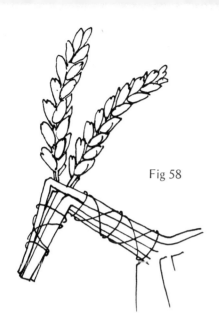

Fig 58

After making the basic shape, you will soon find variations and additions of your own. A corn ear tucked in *under* the muzzle becomes a goat's beard, and extended neck and short rear legs will make a giraffe. Extra padding of straw to the body and chest will make a bull.

The scale of the animal is dictated by the length of the straws, and the larger or stouter the animal the greater number of straws that will be needed. When making large animals, a wire frame is required. If the wires of the frame are attached and bent in much the same way as the preceding instructions for all-straw animals, the straw can be added in appropriate bulk later. If the legs, head and neck are the first to be covered, and the body left till last, most of the ends can be hidden.

Chicken wire is an excellent material to use to keep straw in shape and to give a clearly defined surface and outline. It is much used by thatchers, not only to protect the thatch itself, but to contain and control the animal shapes used as rick finials and thatcher's emblems on thatched roofs.

Thatching is a country craft beyond the scope of this book, but anyone interested in working in straw is bound to observe and take notice of the cockerels, badgers, pheasant, ducks, foxes, peacocks, swans, cats and storks which stand on the ridges of roofs. They once were supposed to ward off evil spirits, or simply to attract the thresher to the rick that was ready for threshing. Today they are popular with birds as nesting material, and the chicken wire outer frame helps to keep their shape intact.

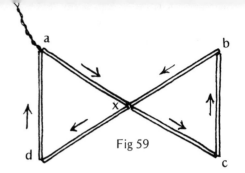

Fig 59

9 Mobiles, Stars and Medallions

Abstract and geometrical designs made of straw to hang as mobiles are Scandinavian in origin. The straw is used primarily as a cladding for framework made of fine wire.

The Swedish Oro

Like the chandelier of spiral plaits, the Swedish Oro is meant to hang from the ceiling, with mobile pendants at its corners. It is assembled from units each made with twelve straws and the units themselves are made from equal-sided triangles. As at least one thread of wire goes through each straw in the design, a large quantity of fine wire of the calibre of 15 amp fuse wire is needed, together with a bundle of very well-matched straws.

The basic unit

1. Cut twelve straws each 4 inches in length.
2. Arrange 6 staws in the pattern shown in fig. 59. Thread the wire through a-x-c-b-x-d, and back to a. Twist the wire together firmly, leaving one long end of wire at a.
3. Make a second pattern as in fig. 60, and thread with wire so that the spare end of wire protrudes from d^1
4. Fold the two shapes as shown in fig. 61 and finally join them so that the wire from a links a^1 and b^1 to b, and the wire from d^1 links d and c to c^1. The result will be a double four-sided pyramid like a crystal model, as in fig. 62.

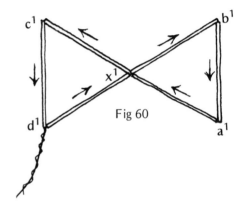

Fig 60

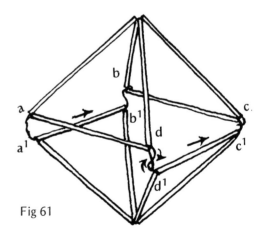

Fig 61

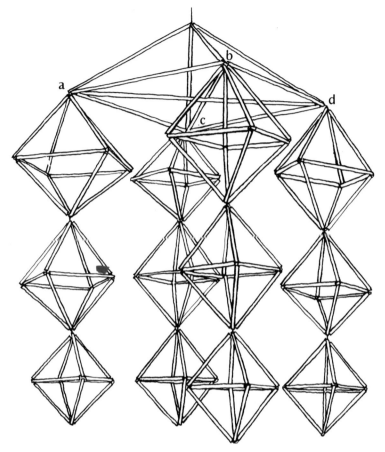

Fig 63

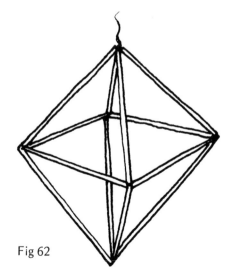

Fig 62

Assembling the Oro

1. Using 48 straws each 4 inches long, make four of the double pyramid shapes.
2. Using 48 straws each 3 inches long, make four similar shapes of smaller proportion.
3. Using 48 straws each 2 inches long, again make four similar but smaller shapes.
4. Take eight straws 12 inches long and make two triangles threaded with wire, threading the two extra straws to join sides **ab** and **cd** in a large single pyramid shape. Then wire in two longer straws connecting **c** to **b** and **d** to **a** as diagonals for strength.

79

5. Make a loop of wire at the top of the large pyramid as a hanger and add the double pyramid shapes in groups of descending size at each of the four corners of this, as shown in fig. 63. The shapes can be tied together with fine thread, as they have very little weight, but the ties should allow the shapes to rotate freely in a slight breeze. Swivel joints as used on fishing lines can be used if preferred, or you can make wire hooks for the junctions so that the shape can easily be taken to pieces for storing without being damaged.

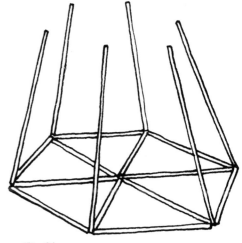

Fig 64

Fig. 64 shows a different shape for the top of the Oro, on a hexagonal base. The flat hexagon is made of three triangles, with sides 12 inches long wired together with three joining straws. Longer straws (16 inches) are wired in with these joining straws, and these come together as shown in fig. 64 to form the apex of the design. The hexagonal variation, of course, has corners from which forms can be suspended, and needs a total of 236 straws. If a group of forms is suspended from the central intersection it will use even more.

For festive occasions, planes of aluminium foil can be added to the figures, giving reflective surfaces which catch the air currents and help the mobile to turn. A point to remember, however, is that the open-work character of the Oro is lost if more than two planes of foil are added to each figure.

Cut kitchen foil to the size of the triangles in the figures, and glue it to the straw with impact adhesive. If the foil is cut so that it overlaps the triangle slightly, it can be folded round the straws, and no glue is then necessary.

A Christmas Tree

A simple Christmas tree can be made from wire-reinforced straws made into right-angled triangles of diminishing size.

1. First make a triangle in the proportions shown in fig. 65, and thread 15 amp fuse wire through the straws so that the ends, tied together, protrude about 1 inch at **b**. The shortest side of

Fig 65

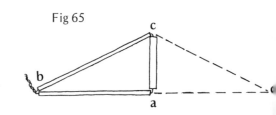

the triangle should be made from stout straw of greater diameter than the rest, for through it must go all the wire threads used to support the tree.

2. Make another triangle next to **abc** (fig. 65, dotted line). Straw **ca** — the central straw — is common to both triangles, and the length of **dc** should match **bc**. Likewise, **ad** should equal **ab**. The threading wires should protrude and be joined at **d**.

3. Make two further triangles with the same dimensions, and the short side **ca** common to both of them. You will now have completed one 'round' of the tree which is shown in fig. 66.

4. Make some more rounds, each consisting of at least four triangles of equal size, but each round smaller than the last.

5. Join all the rounds by placing them one above the other, and threading a flower wire through the central straw from top to bottom.

6. Add a further straw at the top by pushing it over the flower wire which emerges from the top of the tree. You can bind a star or cross of stars to this.

7. At the ends of each 'branch' slip short lengths of straw over the protruding wire, bend them to vertical position as candles, and seal the tops with a small blob of red sealing wax.

Your tree will weigh very little, but it will need to stand in something if it is to stand upright. Push the bottom of the flower wire into an Oasis block, or a piece of polystyrene.

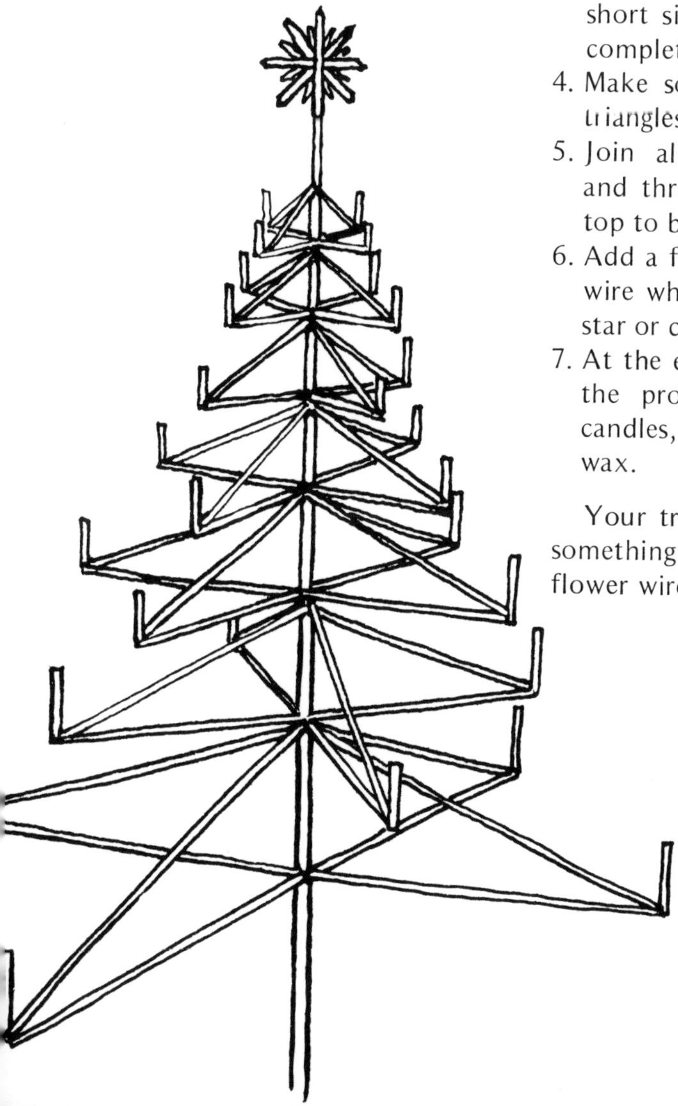

Fig 66. The completed Christmas tree

Six-pointed Star

A simple but effective Christmas star can be made by arranging and joining two straw triangles with sealing wax.

1. Assemble two triangles of equal length on a piece of greaseproof paper.
2. Join the corners with a blob of red sealing wax.
3. Arrange one triangle symmetrically over the other as in fig. 67, and join the intersections with sealing wax.
4. Add bells or small spiral plaits to one of the points of the star, together with holly leaves or a ribbon.

Such a simple ornament is hardly meant to last, but it is very quickly made. Anyone who wants a make more permanent stars must thread the straw with wire.

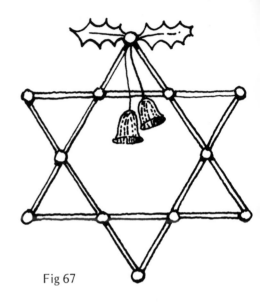

Fig 67

Five-pointed Star

By threading five straws of equal length on to a wire, an equilateral five-pointed star can be made easily by arranging the straws as in fig. 68, and joining the ends.

Multi-pointed Star

Elegant stars with many uses in strawcraft are shown on the next pages. Originating in Germany, they rely for their effectiveness on the combination of different types of straw — some thick, some flattened. Stars and medallions can all be made with waste pieces of straw, including the thicker straws below the first node or joint on the stem — the part the straw-dolly maker discards.

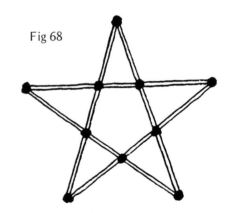

Fig 68

The basic multi-pointed star shown in fig. 71 is made as follows.

1. Take four thin straws 8 inches long, and arrange them like the points of the compass, one above the other.
2. Bind them together with thread at their intersections. The

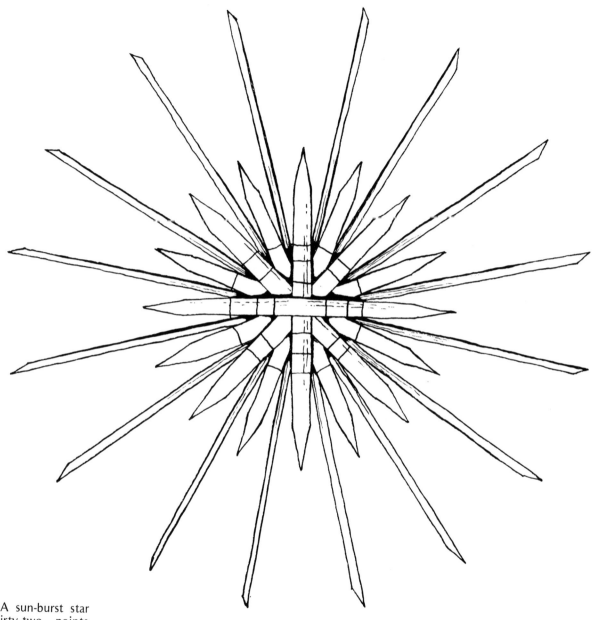

Fig 69. A sun-burst star
with thirty-two points.

thread, taken over and under the straws alternately as shown in fig. 70, will hold the four straws in place. The thread should be woven more than once round this intersection before tying off.

3. Take four thick straws each 4 inches long and flatten them between the thumb and forefinger. Arrange these flattened straws in a smaller series of compass points, and bind them together with thread in the same way as the long straws.

4. Place the small star of flattened straws on top of the large star so that their rays alternate, and bind the two together by the same method as before, over one straw and under the next, until the design is firmly held by the cotton. Draw the thread tight and tie the ends. (The star can be hung up by what remains of the thread.)

5. With scissors, cut the ends of the flattened straws to neat and matching points.

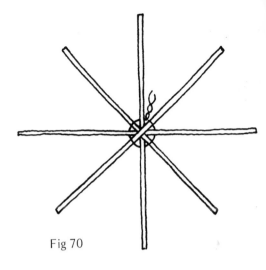

Fig 70

You have made a star with sixteen points. Larger stars can be made with thirty-two or sixty-four points by adding layers of radiating stars or weaving together two stars each made from eight straws. It is not easy to bind eight straws at once — the difficulty is keeping all the straws regularly placed around the circle — and the beginner is well advised to master the simple stars first. The elegance of these shapes is ruined if they are not regular.

A sun-burst star as shown on page 83 is made by winding two four-straw stars of fine straw then two four-straw stars of flattened straws and then combining these two, with the flattened stars lying on the top.

To preserve the symmetry of your stars in the making you may find a piece of composition board or wood studded with panel pins useful. Draw a circle with a diameter of about 4 inches and knock in sixteen pins equally spaced around its circumference. It is easy to make the spaces equal simply by drawing a cross through the middle of the circle, and dividing the angles equally until you have sixteen intersections on the

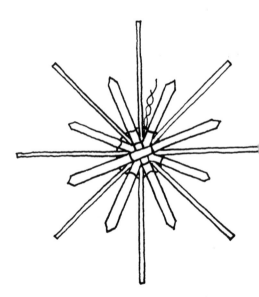

Fig 71. A basic multi-pointed star

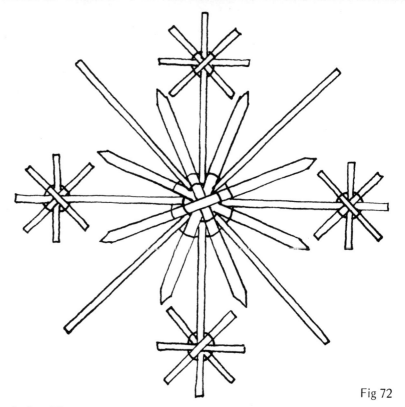

Fig 72

circle. The pins will hold the straws in place while you bind them together with thread as already described.

Multiple Stars

A fine-and-flattened straw star can be made more ornate if subsidiary stars are added to four of the points. Simply cut three short straws of equal length for each of the points and bind them on, using the thread in the same way as before, to produce a design as shown in fig. 72.

Decorated Stars

The elaborate stars on page 86 are based on the multi-pointed star and are made by adding split straws to the points.

Left Decorated stars

1. Make a star with sixteen equal points, or alternate long and short points, following the directions for multi-pointed stars.
2. Take several straws and split them lengthwise into flat strips by running the thumbnail down each straw firmly on a flat surface. Then open out the flattened straw, which will split easily into three or four strips.
3. Curl the strips by running them between the thumbnail and the ball of the first finger, or by pulling them over the blunt side of a knife.
4. Cut the curled strips into groups of equal length, and slide the ends *into* adjacent points of the straw.

The designs can be varied by interlacing the curled strips with alternate points, or by looping the strip around and putting both ends into the same tip.

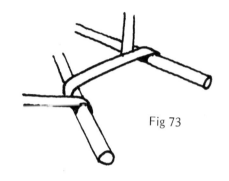

Fig 73

Medallions

A simple but different form of straw weaving is used to make medallions, which cover junctions in straw spirals both decoratively and tastefully.

1. Arrange four straws in an eight-pointed star.
2. Take a fine straw for weaving, and hold one end tightly against the centre. Wind the straw round each spoke of the star in the manner shown in fig. 73. When you have made a complete turn around the circle the end of weaving straw will be firmly held and it can be trimmed off.
3. Continue with the plaiting, adding new straws as necessary by pushing the fine end of the new straw into the butt of the old one, but trimming the length of the old straw so that the join is made at one of the folds, to be hidden behind the 'spoke'.
4. When the medallion has reached the desired diameter, tuck the working end back into the folds at one of the spokes.

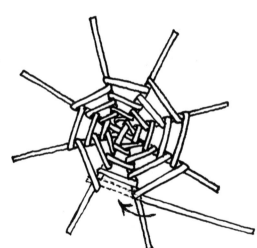

Fig 74. Spider's web medallion. The working straw is tucked in at one of the spokes to finish off.

This weave, called 'spider's web', is useful for a variety of purposes, including many shallow bowls of straw and looks well when combined with traditional spirals.

10 Corn Dolls

Dolls made from the husks of corn on the cob have nothing to do with corn dollies, and although the early examples of American-made corn dolls shown opposite are more sinister-looking than any harvest symbol, there is no real evidence that these were anything more than childish toys.

The examples shown opposite are in the collection of the American Museum at Claverton Manor, Bath, and the one on the right of the picture, standing 10½ inches high, wears a faded pink stomacher and has two added pink bands on each sleeve. The hair is of corn silk and is plaited into a bun. It was made for a child in Oriskany Falls, New York State, about the year 1870. The one on the left is much older, dating from the later eighteenth century.

Such a history tells a good deal about the medium. Firstly it lasts and lasts — it is more durable than wheat straw, less tempting to mice. Secondly, the tough fibrous husks which sheath the corn are easily dyed into colours different from but as interesting as their own natural green and gold; and thirdly that maize has probably been used in America for decorative purposes for as long as the crop has been grown. One authority states that 'the original dolls were made by Indians, who taught the settlers how to make them', but it seems unlikely to me that relations between Indians and settlers would have allowed time for peaceful doll-making.

Left Corn husk dolls made more than a century ago in the United States.

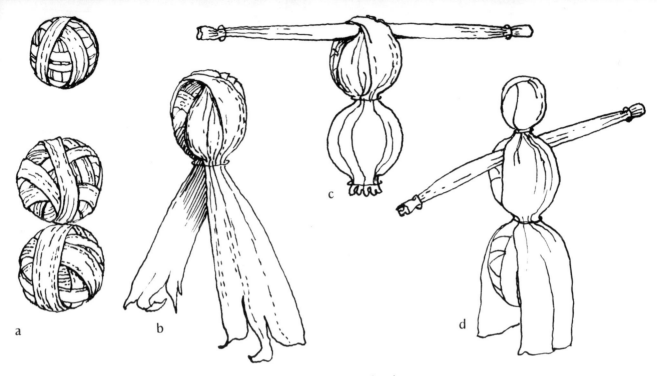

a   b   c   d

If the corn cob is left inside the husks, and the fibrous husks are twisted about it a tolerable mannikin can be made, but it is more interesting to strip and dampen the husks, sort them into sizes and colours and, cutting off the hard ends, use them to build maize figures by the following method.

1. Tear a few leaves into strips about ¼ inch wide, and wind them into balls as you would wind a ball of wool. You will need three balls, one about ¾ inch diameter and two about 1 inch. The ends can be held in place with a rubber band or a pin simply stuck into the ball as each is completed. The smaller ball will make the head, the other two will go inside the body (a).

2. Take one large husk, twist it at its centre and arrange it over one of the larger balls, tying it as in fig. b. Now add in the second of the two body balls, tying below and cutting off the remainder of the husk.

e   f   g

3. Make a tight roll about 4 inches long out of one husk, and tie at both ends for the arms. Slide the arms above the upper body ball and underneath the husk as shown in fig. c.
4. Twist another husk at its centre and with this cover the head, tie at the neck, and incorporate the body, tying at the waist, leaving the ends loose below (fig. d).
5. Add more pieces of husk to the skirt, with the tapered ends upwards, tying them in around the waist and cutting off the husk above the waist. Choose wide pieces for the skirt, and trim them off absolutely level at the bottom (fig. e).
6. Take a piece of husk and tie it tightly around the arm as in fig. e. When turned back on itself and tied at the shoulder it becomes a balloon sleeve.
7. Make a split half way up one husk as shown in fig. f. Place the two free ends over the shoulders and tie both sides back back and front in at the waist to form the bodice.

Fig 75. The finished doll

8. 'Hair' made from the silken fibres which surround the corn cob can be wrapped over the head. It is best to glue this in place and tie at the back in a bun. Further husks can be added to make an apron, a pinafore, a bonnet or a scarf.

9. Complete the figure with a thin strip of husk tied around the waist with the ends falling, if you wish, like apron strings at the back.

There is no pretence that maize figures are corn dollies, or indeed that they are like them. Thus there is no need to limit yourself to a single material, or to remain true to a particular technique. The maize figure can carry a plaited tray made of straw and a plaited carpet beater. She can, like the figures in

Plate 4, wield a broom made of real twigs, or carry a bundle of hay.

Maize dolls can be very naturalistic, and there is a quality about the fibrous material which helps to keep the design simple and clean, so that the result is more than a toy; an example of good folk art.

Since maize is grown all over Europe as well as in America, its use is widespread, and increasing as fresh corn becomes more common as food in the home. The dolls shown in Plate 4 were made in Czechoslovakia. Corn is, however, not the only natural material — a by-product of harvest — which can be used in strawcraft. In the South of France there is a custom of making festival decoration out of palm leaves. Rice, straw, flax, reeds, bamboo leaves and withies can all be used, and all have their strengths and weaknesses, as basket-makers know.

11 Last Words

If you have made all the shapes in this book you can regard yourself as competent in the craft, and you will no doubt go on to design and make many more shapes to the delight of your friends, who will carry them off faster than you can make them.

If you should succeed in keeping a selection of your work, you may want to display it, either in a wall panel as suggested in Chapter 7 or hanging from a wire or against a contrasting material. I have found a coarse network of baler twine a good background to which the dollies can be attached, and from which they can just as easily be removed.

Your collection of corn dollies and straw shapes may increase, and certainly the standard of your technique will improve. Keep your first dolly, as I have done. You will be amazed how quickly your standards rise and this first dolly will prove it to you. It will also be an encouragement to those of your friends who in turn take up the craft.

Further Instruction

Apart from seasonal evening classes, courses are available in Britain at adult education centres. Also, Mrs Lettice Sandford runs a well-known residential three-day course in straw plaiting in August each year at Eye Manor, Leominster, Herefordshire, from which address details are available.

Left The Castleton, a design combining a solid spiral and plaits.

The Dollies of Britain

I am often asked if all the British Counties have their own particular shape or symbol in corn. The answer, certainly, is no, but there are several counties which lay claim to a particular design, and to complicate matters some designs are claimed to have originated in more than one county. This is almost certainly true; the nature of plaiting ensures that certain shapes — like a widening spiral — will form themselves automatically, and the designs they will make will suggest similar motifs to plaiters hundreds of miles apart.

I have myself been surprised, on visiting museums or displays, to find that some designs which I thought I had invented myself are not original at all, but have been plaited for centuries, and probably in several places.

However, the traditional association between Counties and dollies arouses a great deal of interest, and there follows a list of the best known.

Cambridgeshire The handbell, the umbrella
Devon The crown, the neck
Durham The chandelier
Essex The 'terret' (part of the harness for a working horse)
Hereford The lantern
Kent The Ivy Girl
Lancashire The chandelier
Lincolnshire The 'Flycatcher' (shaped like a chandelier)
Norfolk The lantern
Northampton The horn or yoke
Northumberland The kern baby
Somerset The cider flask and apple
Straffordshire The knot
Suffolk The horseshoe and whip, the basket, the bell
Wiltshire The cornucopia
Yorkshire The spiral, the chalice, the candlestick, chandelier
All Welsh Counties The fan

Museums to Visit

Good exhibitions of corn dollies are to be seen at the following places.

Castle Museum, Taunton, Somerset
Ryedale Folk Museum, Hutton-le-Hole, Yorkshire
Eye Manor, Leominster, Herefordshire (from Easter to the end of September)
The Pitt Rivers Museum, Oxford.

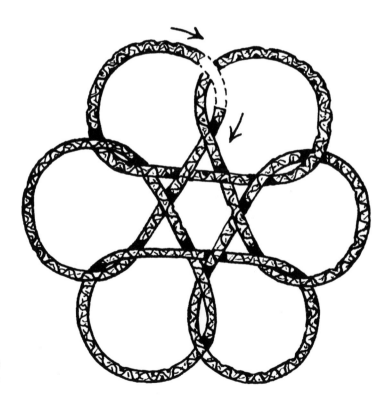

Fig 76. A four-straw plait woven into the 'Turk's Head' design.

Acknowledgments

The many people and organizations to whom I am indebted for generous help and encouragement include the Folklore Society, The Somerset Guild of Craftsmen, National Museum of Finland, Mr George Dabinett, Mr Sidney Beeforth, Mr Joseph Hurst, Curator of the Ryedale Folk Museum, The American Museum at Claverton Manor, Bath, Mrs Lettice Sandford for providing a picture of her wholesheaf dolly, Mrs M Lambeth for help and encouragement and for permission to reproduce her Mother Earth, Somerset House Wedmore for providing a photograph of the Wedmore Wheel and Mrs M Cartwright for permission to photograph the husk face.

The quotation on page 7 by W. Hone is taken from *Golden Bough* by Sir James George Frazer, Part V, Volume 1, p. 264.

Index

Metric Conversion Table

The measurements in the text are given in inches, but for those who prefer to use metric units the following table converts all the measurements in the text into centimetres.

inches	centimetres	inches	centimetres
¼	0.6	8	20.3
½	1.3	9	22.8
¾	1.9	10	25.4
1	2.5	11	27.9
1½	3.8	12	30.5
2	5.1	13	33.0
3	7.6	14	35.6
4	10.2	15	38.1
5	12.7	16	40.6
6	15.2	24	60.9
7	17.8	36	91.4